# Treating Feeding Challenges in Autism

Critical Specialties in Treating Autism and Other Behavioral Challenges

Series Editor
Jonathan Tarbox

# Treating Feeding Challenges in Autism

## Turning the Tables on Mealtime

Jonathan Tarbox
University of Southern California and FirstSteps for Kids

Taira Lanagan Bermudez
FirstSteps for Kids

**ACADEMIC PRESS**

An imprint of Elsevier

Academic Press is an imprint of Elsevier
125 London Wall, London EC2Y 5AS, United Kingdom
525 B Street, Suite 1800, San Diego, CA 92101-4495, United States
50 Hampshire Street, 5th Floor, Cambridge, MA 02139, United States
The Boulevard, Langford Lane, Kidlington, Oxford OX5 1GB, United Kingdom

**Notices**
Knowledge and best practice in this field are constantly changing. As new research and experience broaden our
understanding, changes in research methods, professional practices, or medical treatment may become
necessary.

Practitioners and researchers must always rely on their own experience and knowledge in evaluating and using
any information, methods, compounds, or experiments described herein. In using such information or methods
they should be mindful of their own safety and the safety of others, including parties for whom they have a
professional responsibility.

To the fullest extent of the law, neither the Publisher nor the authors, contributors, or editors, assume any
liability for any injury and/or damage to persons or property as a matter of products liability, negligence or
otherwise, or from any use or operation of any methods, products, instructions, or ideas contained in the
material herein.

**British Library Cataloguing-in-Publication Data**
A catalogue record for this book is available from the British Library

**Library of Congress Cataloging-in-Publication Data**
A catalog record for this book is available from the Library of Congress

ISBN: 978-0-12-813563-1

For Information on all Academic Press publications
visit our website at https://www.elsevier.com/books-and-journals

Working together
to grow libraries in
developing countries

www.elsevier.com • www.bookaid.org

*Publisher:* Nikki Levy
*Acquisition Editor:* Emily Ekle
*Editorial Project Manager:* Barbara Makinster
*Production Project Manager:* Kiruthika Govindaraju
*Cover Designer:* Matthew Limbert

Typeset by MPS Limited, Chennai, India

# CONTENTS

# BIOGRAPHY

**Jonathan Tarbox, PhD, BCBA-D**, is the Program Director of the Master of Science in Applied Behavior Analysis program at the University of Southern California, as well as Director of Research at FirstSteps for Kids. Dr. Tarbox is Associate Editor of the journal Behavior Analysis in Practice and serves on the editorial boards of five major scientific journals related to autism and behavior analysis. He has published three books on autism treatment and well over 70 peer-reviewed journal articles and chapters in scientific texts. His research focuses on behavioral interventions for teaching complex skills to individuals with autism, treatment of feeding disorders, and technology in autism treatment.

**Taira Lanagan Bermudez, MS, BCBA**, is the Director of Feeding Services and Clinical Program Director at FirstSteps for Kids. Ms. Bermudez is devoted to treatment evaluation, research, and the dissemination of behavior analysis, particularly related to behavioral feeding intervention. She regularly presents at autism and ABA conferences and is an author of several scientific papers and book chapters. At present, she directly implements and supervises feeding intervention, as well as telehealth treatment and training of parents and professionals.

# Series Foreword: Critical Specialities in Treating Autism and Other Behavioral Challenges

## PURPOSE

The purpose of this series is to provide treatment manuals that address topics of high importance to practitioners working with individuals with autism spectrum disorders (ASDs) and other behavioral challenges. This series offers targeted books that focus on particular clinical problems that have not been sufficiently covered in recent books and manuals. This series includes books that directly address clinical specialties that are simultaneously high prevalence (i.e., every practitioner faces these problems at some point) and yet are also commonly known to be a major challenge, for which most clinicians do not possess sufficient specialized training. The authors of individual books in this series are top-tier experts in their respective specialties. The books in this series will help solve the problems that practitioners face by taking the very best in practical knowledge from the leading experts in each specialty and making it readily available in a consumable, practical format. The overall goal of this series is to provide useful information that clinicians can immediately put into practice. The primary audience for this series is professionals who work in treatment and education for individuals with ASD and other behavioral challenges. These professionals include Board Certified Behavior Analysts (BCBAs), Speech and Language Pathologists (SLPs), Licensed Marriage and Family Therapists (LMFTs), school psychologists, and special education teachers. Although not the primary audience for this series, parents and family members of individuals with ASD will find the practical information contained in this series highly useful.

**Series Editor**
**Jonathan Tarbox, PhD, BCBA-D**
*FirstSteps for Kids*
*University of Southern California, CA, United States*

# ACKNOWLEDGMENTS

The authors would like to thank T. Carole Eden, Beatrice Baisa, and Lindsey Hronek for their help in proofing versions of the manuscript. We would like to especially thank Courtney Tarbox for her thorough and patient reviews and contributions.

We owe a debt of gratitude to all of the mothers and fathers we have worked with in treating feeding challenges. Your dedication and grit have inspired us to never give up.

# CHAPTER *1*

# Introduction

The goal of this book is to provide the most effective and practical strategies available for clinicians to treat feeding disorders in their clients with Autism Spectrum Disorder (ASD) and other developmental and behavioral disorders. This book uses straightforward language to explain how to implement procedures in real-life settings. In writing this book, we attempted to strike a delicate balance between writing technically enough to satisfy the researchers who will read this book and writing practically enough for this book to be useful to those who work with individuals with autism everyday. When in doubt, we have deliberately chosen to err on the side of practical. For those with the skills and inclination to consume the research literature, the list of references at the end of the book contains a list of research articles not to be missed. The list of further readings in Appendix A also contains review articles, books, and book chapters that are an invaluable resource for treating feeding disorders.

The primary audience for this book is Board Certified Behavior Analysts (BCBAs) who already possess a foundational knowledge of behavioral principles and procedures. However, we assume no previous knowledge or experience with treating feeding disorders. All of the procedures described in this book are taken from research published in peer-reviewed scientific journals. Where research on details is lacking, we draw from our own clinical experience and training we have received from others who are recognized experts in treating feeding disorders and who have worked in leadership roles at feeding centers of excellence, such as the Kennedy Krieger Institute in Baltimore, Maryland and the Marcus Autism Center in Atlanta, Georgia.

A brief note about practicing within your scope of expertise is worth discussing. Most BCBAs work with individuals with autism and most individuals with autism display some kind of challenges with feeding. All of the empirically validated treatment procedures described in this book are derived from basic behavioral principles and

Treating Feeding Challenges in Autism. DOI: http://dx.doi.org/10.1016/B978-0-12-813563-1.00001-X

all are relatively straightforward. One might expect that all of the facts combined together would imply that most BCBAs should be able to treat feeding disorders effectively. However, understanding principles is not enough to make one competent in expertly executing procedures. Like other specialties within applied behavior analysis, treating feeding disorders requires practical experience under the supervision of someone who is already an expert. Therefore, merely reading this book is not going to make you qualified to treat feeding disorders. We highly recommend that you seek out some form of consultation or mentorship, in-person or over videoconference, to help guide and develop your ability to implement the procedures described in this book.

Feeding disorders comprise a continuum, ranging from picky eating all the way to total food and liquid refusal, resulting in complete g-tube dependence and constituting a major threat to health. To treat the most severe cases, you need direct training and ongoing mentorship from those who are already experts in that level of severity. In addition, you likely should be practicing in a hospital setting, or at the very minimum, in close daily collaboration with an entire medical interdisciplinary team. This book is not written for those cases, although all of the procedures contained in this book are relevant for the most severe cases as well. This book is written for clinicians who are treating less severe feeding cases, which constitutes the vast majority of individuals with ASD who have challenges with feeding. There are no black and white rules to follow regarding when a case is "too severe" for you to treat, but a good rule of thumb is that, if the primary feeding concern is medical (e.g., the individual has a feeding tube, the individual's weight is in the bottom fifth percentile, etc.), then you should refer the family to medical experts. If the feeding challenges you work with are not this severe, this book is for you and we hope you find it inspiring and useful.

## 1.1 COMMON FEEDING PROBLEMS

Common feeding problems include challenges with eating and/or drinking that affect an individual's weight or nutrition, food or fluid refusal, food or fluid selectivity, challenging behaviors during mealtime, and feeding skill deficits, among others. The effects of feeding problems range from mild (e.g., missed meals) to more severe (e.g., tube dependence or failure to thrive). Most feeding problems have both medical and social implications. We describe each in greater detail below.

Feeding problems are recognized by medical professionals in the Diagnostic and Statistical Manual of Mental Disorders, Fifth Edition (DSM-5). In addition to eating disorders (e.g., binge eating, anorexia nervosa, and bulimia nervosa), which are less relevant to the subject of this book, the DSM describes Avoidant/Restrictive Food Intake Disorder (ARFID). ARFID is the DSM diagnosis that is most applicable to the feeding disorders covered in this book and the diagnostic criteria are as follows: (1) An eating or feeding disturbance exhibited by failure to meet appropriate nutritional and/or energy needs and associated with at least one of the following symptoms: significant weight loss/failure to gain expected weight, significant nutritional deficiency, dependence on enteral feeding or oral supplements, interference with psychosocial functioning; (2) Not better explained by lack of available food or cultural practices; (3) Does not occur exclusively during the course of other eating/feeding disorders (e.g., anorexia or bulimia nervosa); and (4) Not attributable to other medical conditions or mental disorders.

This book approaches feeding challenges based on observable deficits in eating and excesses in challenging behaviors, not by psychiatric diagnoses. Depending on the severity of the clients you work with, if their parent took them to a medical doctor, they may receive a diagnosis of ARFID, but this has little or no impact on the behavioral intervention procedures that are likely to be effective. This is not to say that the ARFID diagnosis is irrelevant, but merely that it affects behavioral intervention very little. In Chapter 2, Medical and Behavioral Origins of Feeding Problems, we discuss the importance of specific medical assessments and determining whether it is safe for you to work on feeding with a client.

### 1.1.1 Selectivity by Type

Some individuals consume all or most foods from specific food groups and will not eat other types of food. Selectivity by type is defined as an individual "consuming a narrow range of food (often involving rejection of one or more food groups) resulting in a nutritionally inadequate diet" (Sharp, 2016). In feeding literature, foods are generally categorized into four groups: fruit, vegetable, starch (aka, "carbs"), and meat/protein. A client, who is selective by type, might consume foods from only or mostly one food group. For example, he may mostly eat starches or meats and not fruits and vegetables. These clients often eat mostly junk food and only a small number of healthy foods. Despite a diet lacking in various food categories, many individuals with ASD fall within an appropriate range on the body mass index. However, they are at risk for vitamin and mineral deficiencies, as well as diet related diseases, such as obesity and cardiovascular disease (Sharp et al., 2013). Some amount of pickiness with food is completely typical for children (e.g., most children would rather not eat their vegetables), but when the pickiness becomes severe enough to impact the client's nutrition and/or their family's daily functioning, it may be a problem that is worthy of your intervention.

### 1.1.2 Selectivity by Texture

Individuals who are selective by texture are picky about the texture of foods they eat, meaning they more consistently consume foods of a specific texture (refusing developmentally appropriate textures), or that they only eat certain types of foods if presented in a specific texture. For example, Johnny will only eat vegetables in a pureed consistency, not when presented as an age-appropriate bite. Texture selectivity often presents as individuals displaying a preference for baby food or smoothies over regular, developmentally appropriate, table food textures. Texture selectivity is common in children who were born very prematurely and never had the opportunity to breastfeed. In severe cases, children may be 4 or 5 years old and still completely dependent on eating baby food. Such cases often require gradual texture fading and explicit training on how to chew, as we describe in Chapter 5, Treatment Components: Antecedent Variables.

### 1.1.3 Selectivity by Presentation

Some individuals display a strong preference for food being presented in a specific way and refuse the same foods presented in a different way. For example, specific materials (e.g., favorite dishes or utensils), type of container (e.g., bottle vs cup), packaging (e.g., French fries in fast food bag), food positioning (e.g., a separate plate for each food), or self-feeding versus adult spoon-feeding.

### 1.1.4 Food/Fluid Refusal

Another common feeding problem is food refusal, which includes partial or total rejection of foods and/or fluids. Fewer individuals with autism have food refusal than food selectivity (Field, Garland, & Williams, 2003). Food refusal often results in failure to meet nutritional needs, which can result in failure to thrive or malnourishment. Many individuals, with and without autism, whose feeding problem is categorized as food refusal, require medical intervention, including enteral feeding tubes. The two most common types of feeding tubes used for individuals with feeding problems are nasogastric (from the nose to the stomach) and gastrostomy/"g-tubes" (tube inserted into the abdominal wall directly to the stomach). The type of enteral tube used is determined by medical professionals and depends on many individual client factors.

### 1.1.5 Behavior Problems

It is common for individuals with food selectivity or refusal to also engage in challenging behavior during mealtimes. Problematic feeding behaviors include expelling (i.e., spitting food out), packing food in cheeks, turning head away from food, pushing or "batting" feeding utensil away, gagging, and vomiting. Accompanying disruptive mealtime behaviors include crying/tantrums, vocal protesting, elopement, aggression, throwing food or other objects, and self-injury.

### 1.1.6 Skill Deficits

Feeding skill deficits may include lack of chewing skills, poor lip closure, dysphagia (problems with swallowing), and lack of self-feeding skills. These skill deficits can have multiple origins, including individual physical characteristics (e.g., cleft palate or severe overbite causing nonaligned teeth), delayed motor skills or related muscle development (e.g., poor oral motor skills), or lack of opportunities to develop skills (e.g., child only eats baby food, so has not yet learned to chew; cultural preference to eat mostly with hands, so child has limited experience using a fork).

### 1.1.7 Medical Involvement

Whether it be the etiology or the result, many medical variables are relevant to feeding problems. These problems may include weight loss or lack of weight gain, lethargy, and malnutrition. Many gastrointestinal symptoms are often present as well, including reflux, vomiting, diarrhea, and constipation. Such problems can create barriers to growth and development. In some cases, food refusal resulting in medical problems requires medical interventions such as gastrostomy or nasogastric tubes. While sometimes medically necessary, feeding tubes have been shown to interfere with typical oral feeding behaviors (Babbitt et al., 1994).

## 1.2 PREVALENCE AND SOCIAL SIGNIFICANCE

Difficulties surrounding feeding are common in the typically develop-ing population but even more so in the ASD population, with esti-mates of between 46% and 87% of children with ASD displaying significant feeding problems (Ledford & Gast, 2006). It is also worth noting that feeding problems and atypical feeding patterns were part of the earliest diagnostic descriptions of autism (Kanner, 1943).

Although feeding is often thought of as primarily a medical or nutritional issue, the social effects of feeding problems should not be underestimated. Eating a variety of foods, of varying textures, across people and settings is critical to successful social functioning in daily life. Eating in the community is a large part of most people's social lives, including activities like going to restaurants with family and friends, eating at birthday parties, meals at school, snacks at the park, etc. For an individual with autism, who by definition already has social challenges, feeding problems can make social contexts all the more challenging. Establishing the ability to eat in a varied and flexible manner around peers and family can therefore have far-reaching posi-tive effects on daily quality of life for the whole family.

Strengthening healthy feeding behaviors helps to establish lifelong eating patterns. Healthy eating is associated with proper physical growth and development, promotion of fine and oral motor skills, and more successful academic performance (National Center for Chronic Disease Prevention and Health Promotion, 2014). Finally, flexible eat-ing is a source of great pleasure for most typically developing people. In a very real sense, when we help our clients learn to enjoy a greater variety of foods, we are giving them the gift of the lifetime of rich and varied enjoyment that food has to offer. The procedures described in this book, when implemented with proper supervision and support, can help establish a lifetime of happy and healthy eating and therefore have a very meaningful impact on overall quality of life.

# CHAPTER 2

# Medical and Behavioral Origins of Feeding Problems

The vast majority of feeding problems in individuals with autism are primarily behavioral in nature. Like other behavioral challenges, problematic behavior surrounding feeding difficulties generally persists because it continues to be inadvertently reinforced by others in the client's environment. However, feeding disorders often have complicated and interesting origins that were not initially behavioral. This chapter briefly discusses some of the medical origins of feeding disorders, some ongoing medical contributing factors, and then discusses how feeding problems become behavior problems. Finally, we describe practical methods for assessing feeding disorders, both from medical and behavioral perspectives. We also recommend readers to refer to Appendix 9 of Williams and Foxx (2007), which is an excellent resource for assessing feeding problems.

## 2.1 MEDICAL ORIGINS AND PHYSIOLOGICAL CONSIDERATIONS

Many individuals with feeding disorders, with or without autism, were born prematurely. Premature babies often have medical challenges at the beginning of life and many spend days or weeks in the hospital immediately after birth, undergoing a variety of medical procedures. Many medical procedures involve aversive stimulation to the mouth and esophagus. In particular, many premature babies require the insertion of nasogastric tubes (NG-tubes), which are plastic tubes inserted through the nostril and into the esophagus. One possibility is that NG-tubes cause physical pain, and this may lead to oversensitivity of the baby's esophagus to physical contact later, through classical conditioning. In addition, depending on how medically involved the newborn is, the breastfeeding process may be disrupted or prevented altogether. Breastfeeding involves access to warmth and physical contact (primary reinforcers) being repeatedly paired with eating

Treating Feeding Challenges in Autism. DOI: http://dx.doi.org/10.1016/B978-0-12-813563-1.00002-1

through the mouth. It is therefore possible that part of the classical conditioning that makes oral feeding a source of generalized conditioned reinforcement for typically developing babies may be disrupted in premature babies.

### 2.1.1 Autism-Specific Origins

Surprisingly, little is known about why food selectivity is so common in ASD but research has shown that children with autism display more food refusal, more challenges with textured foods, more selectivity by food type, and generally speaking, consume only about half as many different foods, compared to typically developing peers (Schreck, Williams, & Smith, 2004). At least two possible explanations may be responsible for the greater prevalence of feeding challenges in individuals with autism spectrum disorder (ASD). First, oversensitivity to some types of sensory input is a diagnostic feature of autism (American Psychiatric Association, 2013). Food can be a very intense source of sensory input, stimulating the gustatory and olfactory senses the most, but also stimulating visual (e.g., many individuals with autism have strong preferences for what food should look like) and tactile senses (e.g., when picked up by the fingers or touched to the lips). It is perhaps, then, no surprise that some intense forms of stimulation emanating from foods (e.g., strong smells or textures) can evoke very strong reactions from some individuals with ASD (e.g., grimacing and gagging). Certainly, some of these behaviors can be shaped up to acquire operant escape functions (discussed later), but it seems plausible that some of these respondent behaviors may be very real evidence for novel foods being functionally aversive to some individuals with autism, due to their extreme sensory sensitivity.

### 2.1.2 Oral Motor Strength

If a child has never eaten a significant amount of food that requires chewing, it is quite conceivable that their oral muscles are weaker than they need to be to eat normally. However, poor oral motor strength is not a reason to avoid feeding treatment. Quite the contrary, exposing the client to a wider variety of food textures and bite sizes will require her to use the weak muscles repeatedly, which is of course what will make those muscles stronger. If you suspect, or if occupational therapy determines, that a client has poor oral motor strength, it would be wise to progress slowly through increasing texture size and bite size. But this makes good behavioral sense anyway. Gradually fading bite size and texture is likely to make the behavioral intervention more effective and more preferred by the client (more on fading textures and bites sizes in Chapter 5: Treatment Components: Antecedent Variables).

### 2.1.3 Multidisciplinary Assessment

Research has shown that a large percentage of children who have feeding disorders also have comorbid medical challenges that could be related to their feeding problems. For example, in one large study, 38%–69% of children who had food refusal or selectivity also suffered from gastro-esophageal reflux (Field, Garland, & Williams, 2003). For this reason, it is critical for a medical doctor to evaluate the client before you begin a behavioral intervention. As discussed in the introduction, this book is for behavior analysts, educators, speech therapists, and occupational therapists who address feeding disorders that do not have major medical involvement. If it is the very first time that a child has taken a bite of anything edible in his mouth (total food refusal) or if there are major medical complications involved in the child's feeding disorder, the child requires assessment and treatment by an interdisciplinary team that includes medical professionals. In these cases, the responsible thing to do is refer the client out to a highly specialized, usually hospital-based, feeding treatment unit.

In order to ensure it is safe to begin treatment with a client, we recommend that you require the client's parents or guardians to obtain a written statement from the individual's pediatrician or gastroenterologist that states that it is safe for the individual to eat orally. That is, that, there is no medical reason why the individual refuses food, and that, there are no medical or structural variables that could make it unsafe to attempt behavioral interventions (e.g., the structure and/or functioning of the individual's palate make swallowing unsafe). In getting clearance from a medical doctor, it is common that the client will be referred to a gastroenterologist or other medical doctor, who will order a variety of tests, e.g., barium swallow study, gastric emptying study, allergy testing, pH probe, etc.

Sometimes it may be excessive to require the parents or guardians to obtain such a statement. For example, if the client safely eats foods of all different textures and uses age-appropriate bite sizes on a daily basis and whose feeding challenge consists of severe food selectivity by food group (e.g., eating no fruits or vegetables), it can be implied that the feeding challenge is not caused by an abnormality in structure or function. In such cases, the basic behavioral feeding procedures in this book are no more dangerous than presenting edible reinforcers to a child, which is something we do in ABA regularly, without needing clearance from a medical doctor. Some cases are less clear. For example, a 4-year-old child who eats an age-appropriate amount of food, but only in pureed form, and has no history of chewing or swallowing foods that are not pureed. There could be an undetected medical reason why this is the case and you would do well to refer the child to a gastroenterologist for clearance to work on feeding. In any case, if you are not completely sure that you do not need a medical doctor's clearance to work on feeding, you should require the parents or caregivers to obtain it.

We recommend that clinicians implementing feeding treatment become certified in cardiopulmonary resuscitation, including choking interventions, such as the Heimlich Maneuver. Although highly unlikely, it is possible that a feeding client could choke during a meal, which is a life threatening situation if not responded to properly.

## 2.2 BEHAVIORAL ORIGINS OF FEEDING PROBLEMS

The vast majority of feeding challenges in individuals with ASD have at least some behavioral cause. As previously discussed, it is often the case that feeding problems first began for medical reasons, wherein eating or breastfeeding was genuinely aversive for the child because of a history of aversive oral and esophageal stimulation and the resulting classical conditioning. However, like all other behavior, behaviors surrounding feeding have an effect on their environment. If a child cries when asked to eat a food of a new type, texture, color, or flavor, it is highly common for parents and other caregivers to allow the child to not eat it. This reaction, although unfortunate, makes perfect sense. For any child, it will likely not make a significant difference if you let them escape eating once or twice when they cry. However, it is easy for this contingency (refuse food = escape from food) to become a pattern and very quickly become a normal habit for how the parent and child interact around food.

The pattern of parent−child interaction described above is a "negative reinforcement trap." The child's crying or other misbehavior gets negatively reinforced by the parent removing the nonpreferred foods. And of course, it is aversive for the parent to hear their child cry (which is totally understandable), so when the parent allows the child to escape from eating the nonpreferred food, the parent's behavior is then also negatively reinforced by the misbehavior stopping. Like many other problematic parenting strategies, mealtime interactions can become a habit of the parent negatively reinforcing the child's misbehavior and the child negatively reinforcing the parent's behavior of not following through with what they asked the child to do.

If you are a behavior analyst and you are reading this book, you might be thinking this is obvious, and perhaps it is obvious to you, because you have had extensive specific training in this area. If you are a parent or a professional from another discipline reading this book, you may be thinking that we are blaming the parent for the child's feeding disorder, but nothing could be further from the truth. A parent is no more the cause of a child's feeding disorder than a parent is the cause of anything else bad or good that happens with a child. We parents do the best we can with the resources we are given. Some of our behavior affects our child's behavior and we want to know how we as parents can behave differently to help our children be stronger, more independent, and more resilient. The parent's role in feeding disorders is no different. Parents are by no means the cause but, happily, parents can be part of the solution.

### 2.2.1 Escape Function

The scenario we described above was an example of an escape function for misbehavior. The caregiver places a demand (eating a nonpreferred food), the client engages in misbehavior, then the caregiver removes or lessens the demand to eat the nonpreferred food. Research has shown that this is, by far, the most common reason why food refusal continues to occur: because it works to allow the client to escape eating nonpreferred foods (Najdowski et al., 2008). In ABA terms, we say that food refusal behavior, whatever the specific topography (e.g., crying, screaming, and throwing food), has an escape function because it allows the client to escape eating the nonpreferred foods.

It is worth noting that conceptualizing food-refusal behavior as escape behavior is not contradictory to how other disciplines conceptualize it. For example, some may say that an individual refuses textured foods because of sensory defensiveness. When behavior analysts say that a person engages in misbehavior to escape eating textured foods, it is not contradictory with the concept of sensory defensiveness. In a very real sense, the client who has escape-maintained food refusal is trying to defend herself from eating textured foods.

## 2.2.2 Attention Function

A large amount of research has demonstrated that individuals with autism and other developmental disorders sometimes engage in misbehavior to get attention from other people (Hanley, Iwata, & McCord, 2003). Behaviors that are maintained by positive reinforcement in the form of attention from others are referred to as attention-maintained behaviors. The vast majority of research on feeding disorders has shown that misbehavior surrounding eating is escape-maintained, but a small amount of research has shown that some food refusal behaviors may also be attention-maintained (Piazza et al., 2003). It is very common for caregivers to give clients large amounts of attention when they refuse eating nonpreferred foods (e.g., reprimanding, negotiating, pleading, etc.). Therefore, it is a good idea to carefully consider the possibility that attention from others may be part of what is making your client's food-refusal behaviors persist.

## 2.2.3 Tangible Function

Little to no research of which we are aware has documented problematic mealtime behavior of individuals with ASD that is maintained primarily by access to preferred items or activities (as opposed to escape from nonpreferred foods). However, it is very common to see caregivers who have developed strategies that use preferred foods, toys, candy, videos, and so on, to placate their child during mealtimes. It is a small stretch between trying to use a preferred item as a reward to get a child to eat nonpreferred foods and giving in by inadvertently giving the child the item even when he hasn't complied with the request to eat the nonpreferred foods. It is worth being aware of the potential for accidental reinforcement of challenging behaviors when caregivers use preferred items/activities/foods inappropriately during mealtimes, and it may be worthwhile to look out for potentially problematic contingencies surrounding mealtime behavior and preferred items or activities.

## 2.3 BEHAVIORAL ASSESSMENT

Best practices in ABA dictate that we know the nature of a problem behavior before we try to fix it. Put more technically, it is our ethical responsibility to conduct reasonable behavioral assessments before we implement behavioral interventions because treatments based on sound assessment work better than those that are not. Multiple types of behavioral assessment may be needed before treating feeding disorders in an individual with ASD, and we have discussed each below.

### 2.3.1 Indirect Assessment

A variety of questionnaires are available to gather information about parents' or other caregivers' impressions of individuals' feeding problems. Such assessments generally use a rating scale to estimate the frequency and/or severity of feeding behaviors. As reviewed by Sharp (2016), there are five commonly used indirect questionnaires for feeding problems, which are as follows:

1. Brief Autism Mealtime Behavior Inventory (BAMBI),
2. Screening Tool of Feeding Problems (STEP),
3. Children's Eating Behavior Inventory-Revised (CEBI-R),
4. Behavioral Pediatrics Feeding Assessment Scale (BPFAS), and
5. The Pediatric Assessment Scale for Severe Feeding Problems (PASSFP).

Of these, the BAMBI is the only assessment designed with autism-specific content. The assessment includes items that evaluate disruptive behaviors (e.g., head turns, expels, self-injury, aggression, etc.), variations of food selectivity (e.g., prefers same foods at each meal), food refusal (e.g., expels food), and features of autism (e.g., rigid patterns of behavior). Like any indirect assessment, it is important that these measures be used as just one piece of a larger assessment process to develop an individualized treatment.

### 2.3.2 Food Log

As part of the assessment process, we recommend that you have parents complete a food log for at least 3 days. The log should include the date and time, the variety and amount of foods presented, and the variety and amount of foods consumed across several days. It will likely also be beneficial to record the eating location/environment, as well as challenging behaviors displayed during meals

(Antecedent–Behavior–Consequence data collection is ideal). A detailed food log will provide insight into baseline feeding behaviors as a form of indirect assessment to aid in the overall assessment process.

### 2.3.3 Functional Assessment

The effectiveness of feeding intervention will depend on how well you address and match the function of the problem to begin with. As we have said above, most feeding disorders involve mealtime misbehavior that is maintained by escape or avoidance of nonpreferred foods. Escape as a function of food refusal is so ubiquitous that some suggest that you can eschew functional assessment altogether. Indeed, the vast majority of studies demonstrating effective feeding treatments did not conduct functional assessments before treatment. However, at a very minimum, you need to have a thorough discussion with the parents or other caregivers who are most familiar with the feeding problem and ask them what types of behaviors occur, why they think they are occurring, what their usual responses are to them, and what they can do that prevents the behaviors. Usually, an indirect functional assessment of this sort is sufficient. In fact, usually, parents and other caregivers are quite aware that the client uses his misbehavior to escape and avoid eating nonpreferred foods (Fig. 2.1).

You should also backup indirect assessments by conducting a brief descriptive assessment, wherein you directly observe how the caregiver

| Antecedent | Behavior | Consequence |
| --- | --- | --- |
| Mom presents bite of broccoli | Jack swats broccoli off spoon | "You can have pasta instead." |
| Dad presents plate with carrots | Cleo hits head | Given supplemental feeding instead of carrots |
| Grandma presents cup of water | Jeanne cries | Given water in bottle |

*Figure 2.1 Examples of antecedent–behavior–consequence relations for common feeding challenges.*

implements meals with the client and you collect data on the antecedents and consequences of the client's mealtime behavior. This will not only give you good information on the function of the challenging behavior, but also other useful information, such as the usual format for meals, the usual foods and utensils used, and so on. In cases where indirect and descriptive assessments have not provided you with conclusive information about the function of mealtime challenging behaviors, you could consider conducting an experimental functional analysis of mealtime problem behavior (Piazza et al., 2003). Like any experimental functional analysis, you should obtain professional training from someone who is experienced before you implement it.

### 2.3.4 Texture Assessment

If you are planning to work on increasing texture for a client who refuses textured foods, you should first conduct a texture assessment. A texture assessment is a brief procedure used to determine which level of texture your client will currently accept. This will give you data-based information on where to start increasing texture. Terms used to describe different levels of texture in the feeding literature include *puree, table puree, wet ground, ground, chopped,* and *regular.* The exact size and shape that defines each term is difficult to define precisely and is not something that lends itself well to quantifying in a book, but what is important is that you are able to measure texture and create consistent textures from day to day when you are working on accepting textures with your client (see more on texture in Chapter 5: Treatment Components: Antecedent Variables).

To prepare for a texture assessment, prepare foods at multiple different levels of texture. You can use electric appliances, such as a food processor, food chopper, or blender, or you can chop up and crush the food by hand. Generally speaking, it is a good idea to include foods that are not dry or hard, as these will be more challenging for the client to chew. For example, meats, cheeses, raw carrots, and dense breads might not be good choices. To conduct the assessment, present one bite of food at a time, each at a different level of texture. Record which bites the client accepts and which she rejects. Present an equal number of bites of each texture and continue until stable responding at each texture is observed (usually, a few bites of each texture is enough to see whether the client will consistently accept each texture). If the client gags or attempts to swallow the textured food without chewing, use caution and consider using smaller textures or terminating the assessment.

### 2.3.5 Idiosyncratic Assessments

Some individuals with ASD are highly selective in idiosyncratic ways, such as only eating foods of particular colors, sold by particular brands, at particular restaurants, and so on. In these cases, you might conduct an assessment similar to a texture assessment, but where the particular idiosyncratic variable is varied systematically (e.g., each bite is a food of a different color, etc.). Such an assessment may not be necessary if the client's caregiver can directly tell you what variables are of importance (e.g., he only ever eats white foods), but may be helpful for producing data-based information when the influence of idiosyncratic variables is less obvious.

### 2.3.6 Ecological Variables

Many variables impacting feeding are not easily classifiable as either medical or behavioral and seem to be relevant to both. For example, if a client has had insufficient sleep, is over or under-medicated, has a cold or intestinal problems, or is experiencing substantial stressors outside of feeding sessions (e.g., bullying, parents getting divorced, etc.), these factors can have a negative impact on feeding. Ecological variables can often impact feeding as establishing operations. For example, if a client is fatigued or ill, escape from nonpreferred foods may be more valuable than usual; therefore, increasing the probability that she will engage in refusal. Therefore, it is important to carefully assess for and accommodate ecological variables that you can have an influence over, both during assessment and treatment.

# CHAPTER 3

# Preparing for Meals

The previous two chapters described how feeding problems tend to be complex, often medically involved problems. Put simply, the stakes are often higher with feeding than with other behavior problems; poor nutrition, weight loss, and choking are at much higher risk with feeding problems. Feeding intervention also requires more preparation in terms of foods, utensils, etc., than other interventions. In this chapter, we describe practical approaches to planning for the many variables that need to be considered before starting feeding intervention.

## 3.1 PREREQUISITE SKILLS

In addition to being medically safe to eat, there are a number of prerequisite skills that will likely impact the effectiveness of your behavioral feeding intervention, discussed below.

### 3.1.1 Utensil Usage

When you begin working with a client, she may not use utensils to feed herself, either because she has not acquired the skill or as a form of refusal. Some clients who require others to spoon-feed them further require that particular spoons be used. If the particular spoon that the client insists on using is not safe or practical, you may need to use positive reinforcement to teach the client to tolerate the utensils you are going to use before you begin formal feeding intervention. For a client who feeds herself, you will want to ensure that she is able to adequately hold the utensil and manipulate it with food to place a bite in her mouth. Assess this ability with foods that the client readily accepts, not with nonpreferred foods targeted for intervention. If the client is willing to feed herself but cannot execute the skill accurately and rapidly, you may want to choose to have the clinician spoon-feed during the initial phases of treatment and establish self-feeding skills as a later goal of intervention.

Treating Feeding Challenges in Autism. DOI: http://dx.doi.org/10.1016/B978-0-12-813563-1.00003-3

## 3.1.2 Building Rapport

Building rapport is the process of building a trusting, positive relationship between the clinician and client. In technical behavioral terminology, it is the process of conditioning the clinicians on the team to be sources of conditioned positive reinforcement. For example, the clinician can provide the client a bag of preferred toys upon her arrival, pair herself with a highly preferred caregiver during free time, or simply allow the client to engage in preferred activities while she is present, without placing demands. A similar process can be conducted to make the overall eating context more reinforcing. For example, you can leave free preferred snacks out in the feeding environment or complete preferred activities in the feeding environment (e.g., a craft at the table, iPad access in the high chair, etc.). Feeding intervention can be a considerable source of stress and anxiety for the client, and most interventions described in this book involve preventing the client from escaping that stress. It is therefore imperative to be as positively reinforcing as possible from the very beginning.

## 3.1.3 Instructional Control

Prior to beginning the treatment, it is generally a good idea to establish instructional control with your client. This means that your client consistently complies with known instructions. This instruction—response relationship can be established by positively reinforcing compliance with instructions. You may want to target specific behaviors meaningful to feeding, such as compliance with sitting at the table, etc. The specific approach to establish instructional control may vary, but it is generally good practice and will likely aid more successful treatment if instructional control is in place prior to beginning feeding intervention.

## 3.2 TREATMENT INITIATION

### 3.2.1 Age

Early intervention in feeding disorders is preferred over later intervention. Remediating a feeding problem when a client is young will aid in establishing healthy eating patterns that will be carried on throughout that individual's lifetime. In addition to deficient eating patterns and associated health concerns, older clients with feeding problems also have a longer history of reinforcement for poor feeding behaviors.

However, behavioral feeding intervention is effective for clients of any age. And certainly, starting feeding treatment at an older age is much better than not starting at all. An old Chinese proverb goes something like, "The best time to plant a tree was 50 years ago. The second best time is today."

## 3.2.2 Individual Factors

Idiosyncratic variables may influence when to start treatment. Such factors can include beginning treatment during a break from school to allow for more intensive treatment, direct monitoring of side-effects (e.g., allergies and digestive issues), and caregiver participation. If the client is enrolling in a comprehensive applied behavior analysis (ABA) program, it might be wise to wait for a few weeks into the program because the program will likely work on establishing instructional control and building rapport, which may be helpful for feeding. If your client is starting a new medication or is sick, it is best to wait to introduce a new feeding intervention until his behavior is stable. In particular, excessive mucus can exacerbate gagging with new foods.

## 3.3 SETTING TREATMENT OBJECTIVES AND PARAMETERS

Setting good goals and objectives is foundational to any behavioral intervention. We recommend selecting measurable short-term and long-term goals prior to the onset of feeding treatment. Short-term goals should include behavioral benchmarks with criteria for mastery. Long-term goals should include objectives to be achieved further in treatment and/or goals to determine when to discontinue treatment. For example, a short-term goal for a client with texture selectivity who eats only pureed food could be eating a variety of foods in ground form, whereas the long-term goal would be for him to eat a variety of regular texture foods, served in age-appropriate bite sizes.

We recommend working with parents/caregivers to develop your client's treatment objectives. For example, for a child who is selective by type and whose diet consists of only starches and proteins, a goal might be to teach him to eat an age-appropriate number of different fruits and vegetables. However, in this example, the client eats in a separate room from the rest of his family and his mother expressed that she would like him to eat with the family. In this case, you might also include eating at regular family meals as a goal.

### 3.3.1 Target Behaviors

Target behaviors are measured during every meal to determine the effectiveness of the intervention and to monitor ongoing progress. We describe the target behaviors that are commonly included in feeding interventions below, but it is up to you to determine the most appropriate target behaviors for each individual client and individualized feeding intervention.

#### 3.3.1.1 Acceptance

Before beginning feeding intervention, you should determine whether the primary target behavior will be acceptance and/or consumption of bites. Acceptance is typically defined as the client allowing an entire bite into his/her mouth past the plane of the lips.

#### 3.3.1.2 Consumption

Consumption is defined as swallowing the entire presented bite, minus a small residual amount (e.g., smaller than a pea). In order to determine if your client has swallowed the bite, you may need to provide an instruction for him to open his mouth so you can inspect for remaining food. For example, "Say, 'ah'" while modeling an open mouth.

#### 3.3.1.3 Mouth Clean

Mouth clean is usually defined as swallowing the entire bite of food within 30 seconds. You will likely need to use a timer to track this accurately. When the timer expires, check whether the entire bite has been swallowed.

#### 3.3.1.4 Number of Bites Consumed Per Meal

The number of bites consumed is a useful target behavior when the rate of bites is an important factor. It is also a useful estimate for the amount of food consumed; however, the target bite size will also affect the amount consumed. For example, if you are implementing bite size fading (see Chapter 5: Treatment Components: Antecedent Variables) in which small bites are presented, a larger number of bites would need to be consumed to equal the same amount.

#### 3.3.1.5 Self-Feeding

Feeding intervention will follow one of two bite presentation formats: nonself-feeding and self-feeding. Nonself-feeding consists of the clinician using a utensil to present bites of food to the client, usually with infants, toddlers, or young children. The nonself-feeding format lends itself well to nonremoval of the spoon (Chapter 4: Treatment Components: Positive Reinforcement and Escape Extinction). The self-feeding presentation consists of the clinician presenting food on the plate and the client feeds himself. Generally, the bite is prescooped on the utensil and the client is given the utensil. Self-feeding is often a goal of intervention in the later phases of treatment.

### 3.3.1.6 Drinking
Teaching clients to accept clinician-presented drinks may be a goal for clients who refuse liquids initially and teaching clients to take their own drinks may be a goal later in the treatment. Some clients may be bottle dependent for drinks and a goal of treatment may therefore be to fade out bottles and fade in sippy cups and then regular cups. These target behaviors can be treated with the same procedures described in Chapters 4–6 and measured with the same data-measurement systems (e.g., measuring acceptance) described below.

### 3.3.1.7 Problematic Feeding Behaviors
It is very common to encounter a variety of problematic behaviors during the course of any given feeding treatment. These behaviors will vary depending on your individual client, as well as the specific treatment components in place.

#### 3.3.1.7.1 Packing
Packing is defined as food remaining (i.e., more than about the size of a pea) in the client's mouth more than 30 seconds after acceptance. Packing typically involves the client holding the food in the side of his cheeks.

#### 3.3.1.7.2 Expelling
Expelling consists of ejecting or "spitting" food or liquid out of the mouth (i.e., past the plane of the lips) after it has been accepted.

#### 3.3.1.7.3 Gagging
Gagging is usually defined as an observable retching movement of the throat, chest, or stomach, with or without accompanied audible noises. Gagging often occurs during early phases of feeding intervention, especially when presenting novel nonpreferred foods for the first few times. Gagging should still be carefully monitored and tracked.

### 3.3.1.7.4 Vomiting

Occasionally, vomiting may occur during treatment meals. It is a good idea to prepare for vomiting by having clean-up materials easily accessible (e.g., paper towels, cleaning wipes, etc.). Troubleshooting tips are provided in Chapter 9 for how to respond to vomiting.

### 3.3.1.8 Food Refusal Behaviors

We refer to many challenging behaviors that clients may engage in during meals as "food refusal behaviors" but remember to assess function individually.

### 3.3.1.8.1 Head Turns

Head turns consist of the client turning his head away when a bite of food is presented, generally defined as turning the head at least 45 degrees from center.

### 3.3.1.8.2 Pushing the Spoon Away

It is very common to observe clients pushing, hitting, or swatting the spoon away, especially during the early phases of feeding treatment. This behavior is commonly referred to as "batting the spoon away" or "bats."

### 3.3.1.8.3 Crying or Screaming

Another commonly observed refusal behavior is crying. Crying episodes can range from a few seconds long to full-blown screaming and crying tantrums.

### 3.3.1.8.4 Throwing

Throwing food or objects is another potential refusal behavior. We recommend removing any unnecessary stimuli or materials which are within your client's reach. This includes keeping extra food away from the client until it is needed to present a bite.

### 3.3.1.8.5 Self-Injury

Occasionally, clients engage in self-injurious behaviors during mealtimes, including banging their own head against the tray or back of the highchair, or hitting or biting themselves. Obviously, self-injury is serious and must be tracked and managed carefully. We will discuss such cases further in the section on meal-termination criteria later in this chapter.

| Case Examples | | |
| --- | --- | --- |
| **Feeding Problem** | **Target Behaviors** | **Treatment Objectives** |
| • 3-year-old girl with autism<br>• Extremely limited foods: chicken nuggets, cheese crackers, and pretzels<br>• Bats novel foods away | • Acceptance + mouth clean of novel foods<br>• Decreasing batting<br>• Increasing self-feeding | • Add 4 + fruits and vegetables<br>• Eat same meal as brother during family meals |
| • 7-year-old boy with autism<br>• Texture selectivity (i.e., baby food)<br>• Engaged in tantrums and expels | • Acceptance + mouth clean<br>• Increased texture acceptance<br>• Decreased tantrums and expelling | • Eating regular texture foods without engaging in challenging behaviors<br>• Eating same foods as peers in school |
| • 4-year-old girl with autism<br>• Significantly underweight<br>• Ate 1−2 bites per sitting | • Bites consumed per meal | • Eating age appropriate portion in one sitting<br>• Remaining seated for the entirety of a meal<br>• Eating with family |

## 3.4 MEASURING EFFECTIVENESS: DATA COLLECTION

Behavioral interventions for feeding disorders must be evaluated by collecting data during every meal. We will discuss many of the common options for data collection below. In Chapter 7, Treatment Management, we describe how to analyze data as part of the overall process of managing treatment.

### 3.4.1 Trial by Trial

Trial-by-trial data are the most commonly collected data during behavioral feeding interventions, and are collected by recording the occurrence or nonoccurrence of discrete categories of behavior when each bite (i.e., each trial) is presented. For example, in a 10-bite meal, the clinician would record a plus or minus for the behavior of acceptance and/or mouth clean for each of the 10 bites that are presented. Datasheets used for trial-by-trial data resemble those commonly used in discrete trial training in ABA programs. Fig. 3.1 is a sample trial-by-trial feeding datasheet. Each row in the datasheet represents one bite presentation. Generally speaking, one bite or trial on the datasheet begins when the clinician presents a bite and ends when the next bite is presented. Each column contains one behavior that you have to

Date:                Client:              Food pre-weight:         Foor post-weight
Therapist:           Foods:               Start time:              Stop time:

| Trial | Acceptance | | Result | | Feeding behaviors | | | # Problem behaviors | | |
| | 5s | >5s | Mouth clean | Pack | Expel | Gag | Vomit | Head turn | Bat | Food |
|---|---|---|---|---|---|---|---|---|---|---|
| 1 | | | | | | | | | | |
| 2 | | | | | | | | | | |
| 3 | | | | | | | | | | |
| 4 | | | | | | | | | | |
| 5 | | | | | | | | | | |
| 6 | | | | | | | | | | |
| 7 | | | | | | | | | | |
| 8 | | | | | | | | | | |
| 9 | | | | | | | | | | |
| 10 | | | | | | | | | | |
| 11 | | | | | | | | | | |
| 12 | | | | | | | | | | |
| 13 | | | | | | | | | | |
| 14 | | | | | | | | | | |
| 15 | | | | | | | | | | |
| 16 | | | | | | | | | | |
| 17 | | | | | | | | | | |
| 18 | | | | | | | | | | |
| 19 | | | | | | | | | | |
| 20 | | | | | | | | | | |

*Figure 3.1 Sample feeding datasheet, with each row representing one bite presentation. Trial-by-trial data can be collected by recording a plus or minus in each cell or frequency data can be tallied for each bite in each cell. Make your own custom datasheet for each case that captures the most important data for that individual case.*

measure on each trial. Codes such as a plus or minus are written into a cell or the cell can be prepopulated with codes that the clinician circles. The top of the datasheet should have spaces to record the client's name, the date, clinician's name, and the start and stop time of the meal.

The strength of trial-by-trial data collection is that it is easy to train staff in and it resembles discrete trial data that staff are often already familiar with. A disadvantage of trial-by-trial data collection is that it is not a direct measure of the actual frequency of behavior, so it may give only an estimate of the actual rate of behaviors. For example, when you present one bite, the client may hit you five times, but you would only record that the behavior occurred at all on that bite. In that case, no difference in rate would be detectable if hitting occurred five times per bite versus one time per bite. An alternative is to instead tally the frequency of discrete behaviors in each cell for each trial, rather than the mere presence or absence of the behavior.

## 3.4.2 Frequency Count

Frequency data are generally considered the gold standard of data collection in applied behavior analysis but they are much less often used in feeding treatment than in other areas of ABA. To collect frequency data, the clinician merely tallies each behavior that is being measured. The start and the stop time of the meal are recorded, so that you can divide the frequency of each behavior by the duration of the meal, yielding a rate of each behavior. If the cells in your trial-by-trial datasheet are large enough, you can use it to collect frequency data by simply tallying each behavior in each cell, rather than only entering a plus or minus.

An advantage of frequency data collection is that it can be much simpler to collect, especially if only a small number of discrete behaviors are being measured (e.g., bites consumed and instances of the client pushing the spoon away). The ease of frequency data collection, using a datasheet like Fig. 3.2, can be especially valuable when training parents to

### Frequency Feeding Datasheet

Client:                    Therapist:                Date:
Setting:                   Food weight pre:          Food weight post:
Meal start time:           Meal stop time:

Instructions:
- Tally each event in the cell below
- Divide the frequency for each by the total number of minutes to yield the rate and enter rate in bottom cell for each behavior

| Bites presented | Accepts | Expels | Gags | Vomit | Bats / pushing spoon away | Other inappropriate behaviors |
|---|---|---|---|---|---|---|
|  |  |  |  |  |  |  |
| Rate: | Rate: | Rate: | Rate: | Rate: | Rate: | Rate: |

Figure 3.2 Sample frequency feeding datasheet. Tally the frequency that you present bites to the client and the frequency of each of the client's adaptive and maladaptive behaviors.

collect data. A major disadvantage of frequency data is that it can be much more difficult to collect when behaviors are less discrete, are very high rate, or are more drawn-out in duration. For example, frequency data are generally not useful for measuring crying during meals.

### 3.4.3 Weighing the Food

Instead of or in addition to collecting data on the behavior of the client during meals, you can weigh the mass of food consumed by the client during the meal. Generally speaking, it is preferable in ABA to directly measure behavior, rather than its permanent products. However, when that permanent product is the primary outcome of concern, it can be useful to measure. In fact, the actual amount of healthy food the client eats probably matters more than how many bites were accepted. We generally recommend weighing grams consumed as a supplement, rather than a replacement, for directly measuring the client's behavior. In order to ensure that you obtain an accurate measure of the mass of food that the client consumed, do not include any food that was thrown or spilled. Before each meal, you will need to weigh any paper towels, bowls, and plates that may have food on them after the meal, so that you can weigh them again and subtract their weight so that you do not unintentionally count that food as consumed. A major advantage of weighing food as a measure of consumption is that it can be very quick and easy to do. A disadvantage is that it requires a specialized scale.

### 3.4.4 Weighing the Client

We recommend that feeding clients are weighed before beginning feeding intervention and to continue to weigh them at least once per week throughout intervention. For individuals who are underweight due to their feeding difficulties, regular weighing will help to document whether the feeding intervention produces increase in weight. Regular weighing can also help to document the decrease in body weight for clients who are overweight (Fig. 3.3).

### 3.4.5 Interobserver Agreement Data

Whatever data collection method you choose, it is important to ensure that all members of the team collect the data accurately. The best method for ensuring data are collected accurately is by assessing

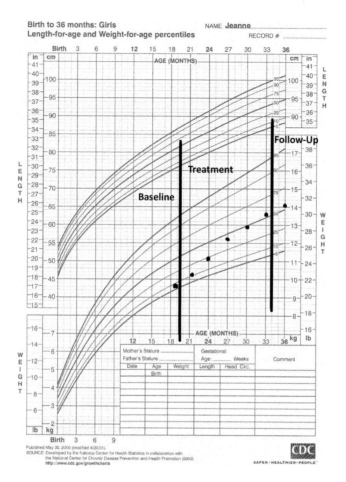

*Figure 3.3 Sample growth chart with client weight plotted about every 3 months during baseline, treatment, and follow-up. Note that the client progresses from about the 5th percentile for weight before treatment, to just over the 50th percentile (i.e., average weight for her age) after treatment.*

interobserver agreement (IOA) (Cooper, Heron, & Heward, 2007). To assess IOA, have two different team members independently collect data at the same time during the same meal. At the end of the meal, the two team members compare their data and discuss any discrepancies. If the two clinicians' data are not in at least 90% agreement, continue assessing IOA for additional meals and continue to problem-solve data collection after meals, until all clinician's data agree to at least 90% of the time. After the team has demonstrated good IOA, continue to assess IOA occasionally in order to prevent "observer drift."

## 3.5 SETTING MEAL PARAMETERS

### 3.5.1 Meal Size/Duration

Meals can end after a particular duration of time has passed, after a predetermined number of bites have been presented, or after a specific number of bites have been consumed. Often, practical considerations regarding family and/or clinic schedule will affect meal duration. Also, consider that, it may be better to keep meals shorter and to conduct a larger number of them throughout the day, so that the client is less likely to satiate during meals. We have often found it effective to begin intervention with meals consisting of only 10 bite presentations.

### 3.5.2 Bite Size

The size of the bite (aka "bolus," in technical jargon) will likely affect treatment and therefore you may choose to vary it across different phases of treatment. If bite-size fading is being used as a treatment procedure (see Chapter 5: Treatment Components: Antecedent Variables), the bite size will start small (perhaps as small as one eighth of an age appropriate bite) and increase in size over the course of successive successful meals. The clinician should determine the target bite size for each session and criteria for moving up in size prior to each feeding session. The terminal bite size is generally an age appropriate size bite and will be the final bite size goal of intervention.

### 3.5.3 Selecting Foods

Selecting target foods of intervention should be done on an individual basis, considering allergies, religious beliefs, and family preference. Consult the family's food log (Chapter 2: Medical and Behavioral Origins of Feeding Problems) for ideas of what foods to target. It is good practice to select foods from a variety of food groups. The U.S. Department of Agriculture (USDA) offers guidelines for healthy eating patterns, including eating a variety of fruits, vegetables, grains, dairy, proteins, and oils (U.S. Department of Health and Human Services & U.S. Department of Agriculture, 2015). A medical professional should be consulted if a client has specific dietary needs, restrictions, or nutritional deficiencies. In addition, it is a good practice to recommend that your client's caregivers consult a professional nutritionist in order to make sure that their food goals align with good nutritional practices.

According to the USDHHS & USDA (2015), healthy eating patterns include:
- A variety of vegetables from all of the subgroups—dark green, red and orange, legumes (beans and peas), starchy, and others
- Fruits, especially whole fruits
- Grains, at least half of which are whole grains
- Fat-free or low-fat dairy, including milk, yogurt, cheese, and/or fortified soy beverages
- A variety of protein foods, including seafood, lean meats and poultry, eggs, legumes (beans and peas), nuts, seeds, and soy products
- Oils
- Limited saturated fats and trans fats, added sugars, and sodium

## 3.5.3.1 Number of New Foods

A good rule of thumb for how many new foods should be mastered throughout treatment is that the client's pickiness should no longer restrict family functioning. It's okay to be flexible enough to allow the client to have a few foods that he just doesn't like and doesn't eat—this is totally typical! As long as you are able to establish a large variety of foods from every food group, it is fine to let one or two foods from each food group go. If there are specific sensory properties of food (e.g., gelatinous textures or pungent meat smells) that are particularly difficult for the client you are working with, it might make sense to avoid these at first. Some sensory variables might not need to be treated ever; e.g., it is not a nutritional priority that a person ever learns to eat meat because they can get sufficient protein and B12 from dairy products. For other difficult sensory issues that will need to be addressed (e.g., runny textures), consider saving them for after you have already built a strong and successful reinforcement history for the client consuming a large variety of novel foods.

## 3.5.4 Fluid Intake

Sufficient fluid intake is crucial for health, regardless of whether someone has a feeding disorder. Make sure that your client has regular access to water all day. If she is significantly underweight, you can consider providing high calorie drinks, such as fruit juices and fortified milk. However, keep in mind that the more calories the client consumes in beverages, the less hungry she will be when you present treatment meals in which you are trying to encourage her to consume a variety of nonpreferred foods. If it is possible that drink calories are interfering with the effectiveness of treatment meals, consider providing only water for drinks between meals or consider using high calorie drinks as reinforcers for consuming nonpreferred foods.

### 3.5.5 Food Preparation

The amount of work involved to cook, store, and potentially transport foods should be considered when selecting target foods, including the type of target foods and the number. We recommend that the client's caregiver supplies and prepares all foods, excluding reheating or applicable texture preparation, in some cases. Foods prepared by caregivers will facilitate generalization to foods the client will be eating in the natural environment and will ensure caregivers are active in the treatment during each step.

### 3.5.6 Meal Termination Criteria

When designing your feeding treatment protocol, you will need to specify the conditions under which the meal should be discontinued. This might include specific client behaviors encountered during session or time limits.

#### 3.5.6.1 Time Cap

The clinician should have a time cap for all feeding sessions that clearly states the maximum duration for each feeding session. A time cap ensures that a meal does not extend beyond what is considered to be an acceptable amount of time for an individual to be required to sit. This criterion should be adhered to even if the client has not eaten the meal. Common time caps are 60−120 minutes, depending on individual factors.

#### 3.5.6.2 Problem Behavior

You may need to terminate the meal if your client engages in challenging behaviors that cannot be safely managed. For example, if a client hits his head hard enough and frequently enough to produce swelling or bleeding and the team cannot prevent it effectively, the meal will need to be discontinued. It is recommended that this type of scenario be planned for to ensure safety, as well as to plan to avoid reinforcing problem behavior. That is, if self-injury serves an escape function, a function-based intervention should be in place that prevents escape and also ensures safety. In the above example, perhaps, alternate demands can be presented, the highchair can be padded, or an additional clinician should be present to aid in the management of self-injury during feeding treatment.

### 3.5.7 Eating Environment
#### 3.5.7.1 Seating

Selecting the appropriate seating should be specific to your client's needs, including age, size, natural setting needs, and protocol needs. The client's terminal seat should be that used in his natural environment, unless modifications need to be permanent. However, when beginning treatment, the team should use the seating arrangement that will make eating most successful. Highchairs, when age appropriate, can be very useful because they are an ethical and socially appropriate means of preventing the client from physically escaping sitting at the meal. Whichever seating option you choose, the client must be able to easily reach the table or tray, without having to shift onto knees or strain.

#### 3.5.7.2 Utensils

When choosing utensils, be aware of the overall size of the spoon or fork (including the handle and reservoir), the material (e.g., plastic vs metal), and curvature. The curvature may be especially important for clients with poor lip closure, in which it would be better to begin with a more shallow spoon. Generally, a spoon is used when introducing new foods, in order to avoid potentially injuring the client with the fork (in which case a plastic or rubberized spoon should be used for the same reason). When teaching self-feeding, consider using specially adapted spoons, with thicker and ergonomic handles and/or divided plates, which have tall side walls for the client to scoop food against. Also, cups with a slot cut out for the client's nose are often helpful when first teaching a client to drink from a cup.

### 3.5.8 Placement

The placement of materials is an important aspect of the feeding environment. This includes planning for spills, distractors, and generalization. When presenting foods, only present the amount necessary for each target presentation, generally one bite to start. Keep additional bites easily accessible for you to present, but out of reach of your client. The placement of your client's seat is another consideration. Plan for whether you want your client on the inside of the table to block elopement, position his viewpoint to best attend to presented food and instructions, and place foods, utensils, and paper towels within your reach. Also, plan ahead to minimize distractions. Whatever environment is being used (i.e., home, clinic, or community) when beginning treatment, remove stimuli in the environment that might distract your client. For example, clear extra materials off the table, including unused feeding materials and stimuli that may compete with your instructions (e.g., others using electronic devices, windows or other visual stimuli unrelated to treatment, people talking, etc.).

### 3.5.9 Feeding Schedule

It is important to make a clear schedule for parents and clinicians to follow that specifies the time of day and frequency of meals and snacks. This may seem obvious but people are busy, especially when parents have more than one child, and it is easy for the daily hustle bustle of life to disrupt planned meals and snacks. Having a written schedule, posted in a clearly visible place in the home and/or clinic, which everyone agrees to follow, will help ensure that all members of the team conduct meals and snacks as planned. There is no right or wrong way to plan schedules. All other things being equal, more frequent meals will likely produce faster effects. Also, we tend to prefer more frequent short meals rather than less frequent long meals, as this seems to decrease satiation and maintain the potency of reinforcers. Still, we have seen excellent results with conducting treatment meals as infrequently as twice per week and as frequently as four times per day, and every schedule in between.

### 3.5.10 Creating a Written Feeding Intervention Protocol

It is critical to have a clear, concise protocol that describes exactly how to implement all procedures during all phases of assessment and intervention. Even if you have a small team and all are familiar with feeding procedures, human memory is inherently imperfect. See Appendices B–D for sample feeding protocols. Feeding protocols should have all of the same components of any good behavior intervention plan.

---

**Components of Feeding Protocols:**
- Client's name
- Date when the protocol was written/revised
- Team members (staff and/or parents) responsible for conducting meals
- Schedule and setting for conducting meals
- Preferred and nonpreferred foods to be included
- Bite size, food textures, and other antecedent treatment components
- Operational definitions of all behaviors to be measured
- Reinforcers to be used and/or preference assessment procedures to determine them
- Consequences for each adaptive and maladaptive behavior

## 3.6 PROGRAMING FOR GENERALIZATION FROM THE START

Generalization is among the most important outcomes of behavioral intervention and this is especially the case with feeding treatment. When we teach a person with ASD to eat a healthier variety of foods and/or to eat textured foods and/or to feed herself, the whole purpose of doing the treatment is to establish the ability for the client to continue using these skills across all aspects of her normal everyday life. The goal is virtually always for the newly established feeding skills to become a new "habit" or "lifestyle." We are not interested in changing feeding behavior that only improves in the presence of the therapist, or only one parent, or only when the specific foods that were targeted during treatment are presented.

Despite more than four decades of behavioral research acknowledging how crucial generalization is (Stokes & Baer, 1977), it is all-too-often still treated as an afterthought. Too many clinicians still take the "train and hope" approach, rather than systematically programing for generalization from the very start of treatment. Fortunately, generalization is not rocket science. Following one basic principle in your intervention will help ensure generalization: Do not do exactly the same thing over and over; build variety into all aspects of your treatment from the very beginning. Think about all of the possible aspects of treatment that the client might get "stuck" on and vary them from day to day.

---

**Ensuring Generalization From the Start**
- Have multiple different clinicians and family members conduct meals
- Use different plates, bowls, and spoons from day to day
- Conduct meals in different rooms of the house
- Vary your language (e.g., "Take a bite," "Have a bite," "Time for a bite," etc.)
- Include many different foods from each food group
- Include many different examples of each food (e.g., not always the same brand, etc.)
- Use many different positive reinforcers, as long as they are all potent

---

Start observing whether or not your treatment is producing generalization very early on. Each time you introduce a new nonpreferred food, if the client accepts the first bite, that is a demonstration of generalization. Celebrate it and consider reinforcing initial instances of generalization even more richly than normal acceptance (e.g., bigger positive reinforcer, etc.). If you are not starting to notice some evidence of generalization within the first few weeks of treatment, consult the list above again and redouble your efforts at introducing variety into the feeding program.

# CHAPTER 4

# Treatment Components: Positive Reinforcement and Escape Extinction

Most feeding interventions that have been shown to be effective in research are treatment packages that contain multiple different procedural components and for which multiple behavioral mechanisms are likely responsible for their effectiveness. In this chapter and the following, we describe each procedural component in isolation; consequence components in this chapter and antecedent components in the following chapter. While you read about each component, keep in mind that very little research has shown any one of these components to be effective alone. Chapter 6, Common Treatment Packages, describes how these various components can be combined to form some of the most popular and effective treatment packages. However, it is important to note that the job of any good behavior analyst is to carefully and thoughtfully analyze which treatment components are the most desirable and likely to be effective for each individual case.

## 4.1 POSITIVE REINFORCEMENT

Positive reinforcement is when a behavior produces a consequence that then strengthens that behavior in the future. Put more technically, positive reinforcement is a response–consequence relation in which a stimulus is added to the learner's environment, with the effect of increasing the probability of that response in the future. Positive reinforcement forms the foundation of all that we do in ABA, and it is generally considered the most ethical first choice for treatment. Therefore, positive reinforcement should always be the first procedure you consider when designing feeding treatment. There may be cases in which it is not necessary to use positive reinforcement (e.g., if lightly salting broccoli effectively increased broccoli consumption alone), but you should still consider using positive reinforcement and make sure to have a good clinical justification if you ever choose to not use it.

Treating Feeding Challenges in Autism. DOI: http://dx.doi.org/10.1016/B978-0-12-813563-1.00004-5

The term differential reinforcement of alternative behavior (DRA) is the most commonly used term in the behavioral feeding disorder's literature to refer to positive reinforcement of eating (e.g., Piazza, Patel, Gulotta, Sevin, & Layer, 2003). The use of DRA in the feeding literature was borrowed from its use in the functional analysis and treatment of problem behavior literature. In other words, mealtime problem behavior is the behavior targeted for reduction and appropriate eating is considered the alternative behavior to mealtime problem behavior. If your primary focus is challenging behavior, this makes sense. But at least to some degree, this term may be a bit of a misnomer in the context of feeding disorders because eating is the central focus of intervention, it is not an alternative behavior. Positive reinforcement of eating is perhaps a more appropriate term, especially since some feeding cases involve little problem behavior and in many other cases the problem behavior is mild enough to clearly not represent the main focus of intervention. Still, the term DRA is the most commonly used term to describe positive reinforcement of eating, so we use these two terms interchangeably in this book.

## 4.1.1 Choosing Reinforcers

In order for feeding interventions based on positive reinforcement to be effective, you must identify powerful reinforcers to use. There are many variables to consider when selecting reinforcers, some of which we describe below.

### 4.1.1.1 Type of Reinforcement

Contrived or arbitrary reinforcers are reinforcers that are not a natural consequence for the behavior during normal everyday meals. Such as, when Hugo takes a bite of nonpreferred food, he gets to play a video game for 1 minute. Other common options for arbitrary reinforcers are brief access to watching TV, a video, brief access to preferred puzzles, figurines, stuffed animals, or other toys.

Natural reinforcers are just what they sound like: reinforcers that are the natural consequence of eating in normal everyday meals. For example, after finishing a meal, a child might get a dessert; or after eating lunch, she might get to go outside and play. Using preferred food as a reinforcer during feeding treatment meals is often a more natural way to reinforce eating nonpreferred foods. In another example, if Sally consumes a bite of carrots, she might get a bite of rice (if rice is established as a preferred food). Consider a common problematic meal, where about half the food on the plate is preferred (e.g., french fries and chicken nuggets) and the other half is nonpreferred (e.g., carrots and apple slices). In many families of children with feeding disorders, a common occurrence is for the child to eat all of the french fries and chicken nuggets first and then refuse the carrots and apples. As a result, the parents likely reprimand, bargain, cajole, and harass the child until finally giving up. To use the preferred foods as reinforcers, the parent or clinician could present the carrots and apples first and tell the children that they can get the french fries and chicken nuggets only after they have eaten the healthy foods. In order to make the meal more likely to be successful early on, the parent or clinician can divide each food item into bite sizes and give one bite of preferred food as a reinforcer for each bite of nonpreferred food eaten. At first, it may be necessary to use very highly preferred foods as the reinforcers, such as candy or small bites of dessert items.

The benefits of using preferred foods as reinforcers are that this might be perceived as a more "common sense" type of reinforcement to many parents as it mimics a "meal-then-dessert" relationship and it may be more similar to what a meal may look like in the natural environment. In addition, it will likely be easier to provide preferred foods as reinforcement given that most meals take place in dining areas near kitchens, where access to preferred foods is easier. Further, there is no need to disrupt the meal in order to deliver the reinforcer and it eliminates the need to take away a reinforcer, such as a computer tablet. Finally, bites of preferred foods may be consumed more quickly than the duration of time that you might need to give the client access to an arbitrary reinforcer, which can make meals more efficient. Whether it be arbitrary reinforcers or preferred food as reinforcers, any effective reinforcement, by definition, will result in the increased consumption of nonpreferred foods.

### 4.1.1.2 Preference Assessment

Preference assessments are procedures used to determine which foods or items are preferred by the learner in order to determine which are likely to work as positive reinforcers. Ample research has shown that items identified through preference assessments are far more likely to be effective as reinforcers than items identified by clinician or parent opinion alone. To conduct a preference assessment to determine which foods are preferred and nonpreferred, you can begin by asking care-givers who are familiar with the client's preferences. Make a list of foods the caregiver reports that the learner likes (if any), foods that he doesn't necessarily like but might eat, and foods he consistently does not eat (healthy ones that the parents want the client to learn to eat). To conduct the assessment, present an equal number of bites of each food, one food at a time, and record whether the client consumes the food. Typically, neither reinforcement for consumption nor escape extinction for refusal behavior is implemented during preference assess-ments. Simply present the bites and do not deliver any differential con-sequences based on the client's behavior.

Continue presenting bites until stable levels of responding are observed with each food. Foods that are consumed in most or all of the trials in which they were presented are likely not in need of inter-vention. Foods that are consumed 100% of the time, and which the caregivers report are highly preferred, are good candidates to use later for positive reinforcement for eating nonpreferred foods. Foods that are consumed rarely or never are good candidates to target during intervention (see setting treatment goals in Chapter 3: Preparing for Meals). Foods that are consumed approximately half of the time may be good candidates for early target foods during intervention because they may be easier for the client to be successful with in the beginning.

### 4.1.1.2.1 Multiple Stimulus Without Replacement Preference Assessment

Multiple options exist for conducting preference assessments to deter-mine which items to use as positive reinforcers for eating nonpreferred foods. An easily administered preference assessment is the multiple stimulus without replacement (MSWO) procedure (DeLeon & Iwata, 1996). To complete an MSWO preference assessment, 3−7 items are presented in an array. The client is told to "pick one" and then allowed to play with/consume the item for approximately 30 seconds. That item is then removed from the array for the rest of the assessment and the remaining items are presented for the client to select again. The order in which each item was chosen is recorded and the earlier an item is chosen, the more likely it is to be an effective reinforcer, com-pared to the others. In order to increase the accuracy of the assess-ment, you can repeat it once or twice and average the data. It is generally recommended that foods and nonedible items (e.g., toys) be presented in separate assessments, or choose to assess only edibles or nonedibles.

### 4.1.1.2.2 Frequent Mini Preference Assessments

Completing an MSWO preference assessment, including one or more repetitions of the assessment, is a highly effective method for identifying potential reinforcers, but it can be time consuming and you are therefore not likely to do it often. An excellent alternative is to conduct a one-trial mini assessment before every meal, in which only two or three items are presented and the item chosen first is then used as the reinforcer until the next mini preference assessment is conducted before the next meal.

## 4.1.2 Reinforcement Schedules

The feeding intervention should clearly specify when and how much reinforcement should be provided, referred to as the "schedule of reinforcement." Continuous reinforcement schedules provide reinforcement following every instance of the target behavior. For example, the client receives one bite of preferred food following each bite of nonpreferred he accepts. Continuous reinforcement is also referred to as a Fixed Ratio 1 schedule of reinforcement. In contrast, intermittent schedules of reinforcement specify how only some of the responses will result in a reinforcer. Intermittent reinforcement can be delivered after the client eats a fixed number of bites (e.g., the client receives reinforcement after every 5 bites he accepts) or a varied schedule of reinforcement, delivered after a varied number of responses (e.g., the client receives reinforcement after approximately 5 bites, ranging from 3 to 7).

To maximize effectiveness at the beginning of the treatment, use a denser schedule of reinforcement, so that varied and flexible eating is richly reinforced. After the client's eating has reliably improved, consider changing to intermittent reinforcement. Gradually decreasing the frequency of reinforcement is referred to as "schedule thinning," described in Chapter 6, Common Treatment Packages and Chapter 8, Caregiver Training and Follow-Up.

## 4.1.3 Magnitude/Duration

The magnitude of reinforcement refers to the size or amount of reinforcement that is provided each time a reinforcer is delivered. Traditionally, when using tangible reinforcers in feeding intervention, the client is given the reinforcer for 30 seconds after accepting or consuming a bite. However, the magnitude of reinforcement can be increased to maximize the effectiveness of treatment or decreased to fade out treatment. With edible reinforcers, the physical amount of the reinforcer can be manipulated. For example, when a client takes a bite of broccoli, she then receives one bite of brownie, versus two bites, etc. There is no rule about what magnitude of reinforcement to use, other than that it must be large enough to be effective. However, larger reinforcers increase satiation to a greater degree, so consider using the smallest magnitude of reinforcement that is still highly effective.

## 4.1.4 Reinforcement Contingencies

Once a target desirable feeding behavior has been selected, reinforcement contingencies can be planned to strengthen it. Reinforcement contingencies should be selected based on your current treatment objectives and can be changed throughout treatment, depending on what works for each individual client.

### 4.1.4.1 DRA for Acceptance

Differential reinforcement of acceptance consists of providing reinforcement immediately following acceptance of a bite. If the only treatment component you are implementing is positive reinforcement for eating, then challenging behaviors do not affect the contingency. For example, if the client accepts the bite while turning his head, or accepts and then expels, he stills earns the reinforcer.

### 4.1.4.2 DRA for Consumption

Differential reinforcement of consumption consists of providing reinforcement for eating the bite. Most often, DRA for mouth clean is implemented in which reinforcement is provided for swallowing the bite within 30 seconds. This is the standard in most of the feeding literature and works well to teach your client to eat efficiently. However, differential reinforcement of swallowing (i.e., swallowing the bite at any time, even if it takes longer than 30 seconds) can also be effective.

### 4.1.4.3 DRA for Related Skills

Reinforcement can also be provided for other related behaviors you would like to increase. Behaviors such as chewing, staying in seat, etc. are often important to address in order to progress toward treatment objectives, or may be treatment objectives themselves; thus, they too can be targets for positive reinforcement.

| Sample feeding problem | Target behavior | Potential intervention |
|---|---|---|
| Selectivity by type (e.g., eats no fruits/vegetables) | Acceptance of novel foods | o  DRA of acceptance<br>o  Size fading<br>o  Texture fading |
| Selective by texture (e.g., eats only baby food) | Acceptance of various textures | o  DRA of acceptance<br>o  Texture fading<br>o  Size fading |
| Selectivity by presentation (e.g., bottle dependent) | Acceptance of various vessels/containers | o  DRA of acceptance |
| Expels bites | Mouth clean | o  DRA of mouth clean<br>o  DRA of mouth clean + escape extinction<br>o  Representation of bites |
| Packs bites | Mouth clean | o  DRA of mouth clean<br>o  DRA of mouth clean + escape extinction<br>o  Redistribution of bites |
| Eats very small portions | Number of bites/amount consumed | o  DRA of meal |
| Behavior problems during meals | Acceptance of novel foods | o  DRO of challenging behavior |
| Skill deficit (e.g., lack of chewing) | Skill (e.g., chewing) | o  DRA of skill<br>o  DRA of mouth clean<br>o  Texture fading |

Figure 4.1 Sample feeding problems, target behaviors, and potentially useful interventions.

#### 4.1.4.4 Differential Reinforcement of Other Behavior

Differential reinforcement of other behavior (DRO) can be utilized to decrease instances of challenging behaviors, such as expelling, gagging, or vomiting. It is most common to simply ignore these behaviors but DRO can be used instead. For example, you might give the client 1 minute access to an IPad for every 5 minutes she has not cried during a meal (Fig. 4.1).

## 4.2 ESCAPE EXTINCTION

Food refusal behaviors persist because they work. Of course, every individual is different and a careful assessment should be conducted to determine whether the function of food refusal really is avoidance of eating nonpreferred foods. But research has shown that the vast majority of food refusal behaviors persist because they help the individual to get out of eating the foods she does not want to eat (Najdowski et al., 2008). That is why escape extinction, which is defined as preventing the food refusal behavior from resulting in escape and avoidance of eating, is the most important and most research-proven technique for decreasing food refusal and increasing consumption of new foods. Most of the other procedures described in this book can be thought about as supplementary procedures that make feeding treatment work more quickly, be more highly preferred by the client and caregivers, and can make the whole process more fun for everyone. But in the vast majority of cases, the behavioral principle of escape extinction is what makes a treatment work. Fortunately, this means that you may likely have more leeway with modifying and customizing procedures to make them a good fit for a particular client or family, as long as you ensure that the client cannot escape eating nonpreferred foods by refusing to eat them.

## 4.2.1 Procedural Variations of Escape Extinction

Like any other behavioral intervention procedure, escape extinction is defined functionally (whether or not it is actually placing refusal behavior on extinction), not topographically (what the procedure looks like). Different forms of escape extinction for food refusal, at first sight, appear very different. That is because they are indeed topographically very different, but functionally, any procedure that prevents food refusal from resulting in escape or avoidance of eating, is functionally the same. Parents, clients, and staff may have strong preferences for some procedures over others and some procedures may work faster than others. Below, we describe some of the main variations of escape extinction.

### 4.2.1.1 Nonremoval of the Spoon

Nonremoval of the spoon is the most research-proven and most commonly used escape extinction procedure in feeding treatment. The most commonly used method for implementing nonremoval of the spoon is to present a bite of food to the client and hold it immediately in front of (but usually not touching) his lips, and he is asked to, "Take a bite" (Piazza, Patel, Gulotta, Sevin, & Layer, 2003). The spoon is held in place continuously until he accepts the bite into his mouth. Challenging behaviors, such as crying, screaming, turning the head away, pushing or hitting the spoon away, or hitting the clinician, are supposed to result in no consequence; the spoon is supposed to stay in place immediately in front of the client's lips. If the client turns his head, the spoon follows so that it remains immediately in front of the mouth. In practice, this often requires one adult to hold the spoon and another adult to block the client's attempts to hit or push the spoon (without manually restraining the client). If the bite of food is spilled off the spoon, the clinician immediately scoops up another bite and replaces it at the client's lips. The meal can either be continued indefinitely until the client takes the bite or until bedtime (whatever comes first) or terminated after a predetermined duration of time passes without taking a bite (e.g., 60 minutes). See more on meal termination criteria in Chapter 3, Preparing for Meals.

When implementing nonremoval of the spoon, some clinicians choose to insert the bite of food into the client's mouth any time the client opens his mouth, including when he opens it to protest. Other clinicians choose to only insert the spoon into the client's mouth when the client opens his mouth to accept the bite. We recommend doing the latter; however, many clinicians report that the former approach is highly effective. No research, of which we are aware, has compared the two options.

### 4.2.1.1.1 Advantages
Nonremoval of the spoon has at least two major advantages. First, a very large amount of research has shown that it works. So if you want a procedure that is the most likely to be successful, based on research, this is it. Second, it works quickly. Most individuals begin accepting new foods within the first few meals in which the procedure is used. If you have a short amount of time to work on feeding or if the family is in serious crisis and is considering much more intrusive alternatives (e.g., insertion of a feeding tube), nonremoval of the spoon might be the best choice as it is the most likely to work quickly. One possible reason that it works quickly is that clients often take their first bite of nonpreferred food within the first meal and so they contact large positive reinforcement contingencies for acceptance very early on. Other treatment approaches often do not result in the client taking their first bite for many meals or not at all, until nonremoval of the spoon is added.

### 4.2.1.1.2 Disadvantages
Nonremoval of the spoon has at least two major disadvantages. First, it can be very labor-intensive. As mentioned above, it may require two adults to implement. It is often possible to recruit and train one of the client's parents or other caregivers to assist in implementing the

procedure. An advantage of this is that it builds in some amount of parent training from the start, so you will need to spend less time and effort training parents later. A disadvantage is that parents may prefer not to have to assist in a difficult and emotionally upsetting intervention right from the start.

A second and more important disadvantage of nonremoval of the spoon is that it is intrusive. By definition, you are putting a highly nonpreferred stimulus directly in the client's face. Imagine if someone put something you truly hate directly in your face and they would not move it. Nonremoval of the spoon is probably among the most intrusive ABA interventions that are still considered appropriate. It is no surprise that most individuals with food selectivity do not prefer the procedure and it is no surprise that the procedure often evokes challenging behavior. For these reasons, staff and family members often report that they do not like implementing nonremoval of the spoon and they would rather not do it if they do not have to.

However, it is also worth noting that severe food selectivity can have very serious consequences for an individual's nutrition and societal and familial adjustment. When deciding whether to use nonremoval of the spoon with the client's family and other stakeholders, you should have a frank conversation about intrusiveness and the very high likelihood of the client displaying severe challenging behavior and the emotional effects that will have on family members. The authors of this book have never met a family who would rather their child's feeding disorder continue than implement nonremoval of the spoon. In other words, the negative side effects of nonremoval of the spoon can be significant, but they are rarely worse than allowing the problem to go untreated. Still, many staff and family would rather implement nonremoval of the spoon as a last resort after exhausting several reinforcement and antecedent-based procedures first. Fortunately, there are several other ways in which food refusal can be placed on escape extinction, which we shall now describe.

### 4.2.1.2 Nonremoval of the Meal

"Nonremoval of the meal" (Tarbox, Schiff, & Najdowski, 2010), which has also been described as a "meal termination criteria" procedure, is *functionally* very similar to nonremoval of the spoon; the demand to eat the nonpreferred food is not discontinued until the client consumes the bite. But *topographically*, the two procedures are very different. Rather than the spoon being placed immediately in front of the client's face (which can be quite intrusive), the food is made available in some other way and the client is not allowed to leave the meal setting until she consumes the required amount. For individuals who can self-feed, foods may be placed on a bowl or plate within their reach and the client can then feed herself a bite with a spoon or her fingers, when she chooses to consume a bite. If the client throws the food or utensils or otherwise makes a mess, you replace the materials on the table, perhaps out of reach this time. The client can then reach for it or otherwise indicate to you when she is choosing to take a bite from it. You may start with only requiring one bite of nonpreferred food before the meal is terminated and the client can go have fun with something else. You may then gradually increase the amount of food on the plate, thus requiring the client to consume more and more nonpreferred foods, until an age-appropriate, healthy meal is eventually consumed at each meal (see Chapter 5: Treatment Components: Antecedent Variables, for more on demand fading).

For individuals who do not have the skill to feed themselves, the clinician can present a bite within view but not immediately in front of the client's face. For example, you could sit across a table from the client, hold up a bite of food from across the table, and say "I have a bite of broccoli here for you. Take a bite." When the client opens her mouth to accept the bite, then you bring the spoon close enough for her to accept it into her mouth.

Nonremoval of the meal is much more convenient to implement when the client is young enough to sit in a highchair because highchairs make it easy to physically control when the client is allowed to leave the meal (when he has consumed the required amount of nonpreferred food for that meal). For clients not in a highchair, you will need to identify how you are going to prevent them from leaving the meal. It often works to use verbal and partial physical prompts to guide the client back to his chair when he gets up. Be careful not to use too much verbal prompting, as you may inadvertently reinforce the behavior with attention, thereby shaping up an additional attention function for inappropriate behavior. Some individuals may attempt to escape sitting in their chair with enough force that it is not safe or feasible to continue to prompt them to sit back in their chair. If this is the case, you need to ensure that the individual cannot access anything else that he prefers while being absent from the meal. For example, he may insist on sitting on the kitchen floor and that may not be problematic for the treatment to still be effective, as long as you do not allow him to do anything else that is reinforcing while sitting on the floor (e.g., prevent access to electronic devices or other reinforcers, do not play with or engage the individual in conversation, and so on).

It is also important to emphasize being safe and reasonable when implementing nonremoval of the meal. Just like any other intervention, you need to do whatever it takes to maintain a safe and dignified treatment environment for the client. If the client needs to use the bathroom while she is refusing to eat during a meal, you need to take her to the bathroom. Simply take her back to the chair or highchair when she is done in the bathroom. If the individual engages in self-injury and you are not able to prevent injury while she is seated in the chair or highchair, then you may need to use padding or protective equipment or you may need to remove her from the chair or highchair and plan better for the next meal. If the client has specialized seating or back/neck support needs because of an injury or disability, these obviously need to be accommodated while you implement nonremoval of the meal.

### 4.2.1.2.1 Advantages and Disadvantages

Most (but not all) people will view nonremoval of the meal as less intrusive than nonremoval of the spoon because it does not require you to put something that the client finds aversive immediately in front of their face. No research, of which we are aware, has compared the two procedures, but in our experience, nonremoval of the meal occasions fewer and less intense extinction bursts and escape behavior. Nonremoval of the meal is also sort of a common sense approach. It's much like what one's grandmother might tell you: "You can just sit there till you are done with dinner." A disadvantage is that it may take a long time. At least in the first few meals, clients may wait a long time to take the first bite. Some parents may find it too intrusive to require a client to remain at a meal for an hour or more.

## 4.2.2 When Escape Extinction is Not Possible

Sometimes, due to practical or safety reasons, full escape extinction is not possible. That is, when the client refuses nonpreferred foods, you may sometimes need to allow them to escape, regardless of what variation of escape extinction you attempt. If this is the case, you may need to overcompensate for your inability to fully do extinction by substantially increasing the amount of reinforcement you are delivering for eating and minimizing, to the greatest extent possible, the escape for food refusal. For example, if you cannot leave the spoon in front of the client's face because of severe behavior, you could give the client a minimal amount of escape from the spoon (e.g., 5 or 10 seconds of escape) when he hits or cries but give him a much larger reinforcer (e.g., 10 minutes of escape from the meal) when he eats a bite of new foods. Or, you could arrange a meal where if the client refuses to eat a new food, he gets a small amount of neutral food, whereas if he accepts a small amount of new food, he gets a large amount of highly preferred foods. Modifications such as these will likely make the treatment process take longer. However, if they work, they may be able to be faded out gradually and they may sometimes be your only options for effective treatment.

## 4.2.3 Combining Reinforcement and Extinction

Positive reinforcement and escape-extinction procedures were described in separate sections for the sake of clearly describing each individual treatment component but it is rarely effective to implement positive reinforcement without escape extinction and it is rarely ethical to implement escape extinction without positive reinforcement. Therefore, for each individual case, you will likely need to analyze and design the optimal combination of treatment components. Chapter 6, Common Treatment Packages, describes several common treatment packages.

# CHAPTER 5

# Treatment Components: Antecedent Variables

Antecedent variables are any aspect of the feeding treatment that you implement before the client has the opportunity to either eat or refuse food. In technical behavioral terms, they are antecedent environmental stimuli or motivating operations that decrease the probability of challenging behaviors and increase the probability of consuming nonpreferred foods. The behavioral feeding research literature has shown that a large number of antecedent variables can be helpful in treating feeding disorders. However, very few studies have shown any antecedent variables to be effective treatments when implemented alone. In particular, most published studies have shown that the antecedent components in this chapter require some form of escape extinction to be implemented at the same time, in order for the overall treatment to be effective. Therefore, while reading this chapter, it will be useful to consider how these antecedent components might be combined with positive reinforcement and escape extinction when working with the clients you treat. In addition, Chapter 6, Common Treatment Packages provides practical descriptions of some of the more common treatment packages.

## 5.1 EXPOSURE

It is possible that, in a small percentage of cases, mere exposure to novel foods may increase acceptance of those foods. For parents and caregivers, this can be an easy and practical way to start introducing new foods. Provide frequent availability of novel foods to the client, perhaps by simply leaving foods out and available. For example, instead of having a candy bowl on the coffee table, have a bowl of fruit. Since this procedure is merely exposure and you will not be following through with a request to eat, do not ask the client to consume the foods. The foods can be left out and/or the client can be shown them, e.g., "Look, yummy apples."

Treating Feeding Challenges in Autism. DOI: http://dx.doi.org/10.1016/B978-0-12-813563-1.00005-7

## 5.2 HUNGER

The technical behavioral term for hunger is food deprivation, in that the client has not eaten for some period of time before a meal, which is the environmental condition that produces hunger. It is important to note that the term "deprivation" means something very different in technical behavioral jargon than it does in daily usage. It does NOT mean depriving the client of necessary nutrition or calories. It simply means ensuring that the client has not eaten in the last 2 or 3 hours before a treatment meal. Little research has evaluated the effects of hunger on the effectiveness of behavioral interventions for feeding disorders. However, until more conclusive research is conducted, we recommend asking parents to make sure the client is hungry before treatment meals. Obviously, if your client is medically fragile and/or is severely underweight, such recommendations should be approved by a medical doctor and it is always wise to weigh the client frequently to ensure she is not losing weight.

## 5.3 BITE SIZE

The size of the bite (or bolus in technical jargon) that you present during meals should be planned prior to initiating the feeding session and it can have a strong influence on the effectiveness of an intervention. *Stimulus fading* is the technical behavioral term that is defined as systematically altering the physical properties of a stimulus. In the case of bite size, stimulus fading refers to gradually fading the bite size up or down across successive meals. For optimal effectiveness, bites are first presented at a very small size (e.g., a pea or smaller). As the client is successful, the bite size is then systematically faded up until the terminal bite size (often an age-appropriate bite size) is reached. For example, if Margo is learning to eat chicken, treatment may start with pea-sized bites of chicken. Once she is consistently eating pea-sized bites, the bite size may be faded up to the size of a dime, then a quarter, etc. (Fig. 5.1).

One practical way of cutting up bites when preparing for meals is to first prepare an age-appropriate bite size and then cut that in half. Then you can cut each of those halves in half, creating four quarters. Then each of those can be cut in half, creating 8 eighths of a bite. In extreme cases, you can cut each of those in half, creating 16 sixteenths of a bite. There is usually no need to be overly-obsessive about making

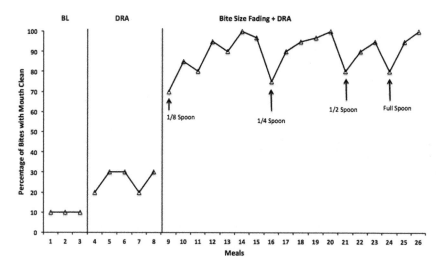

*Figure 5.1 Sample graph of a DRA treatment that did not increase consumption adequately. Adding bite size fading, gradually fading from one-eighth bite size to full size, effectively increased consumption.*

sure that what is called a particular size (e.g., quarter bite) is always *exactly* the same from meal to meal or from clinician to clinician, but at least a reasonable amount of consistency will help decrease variability in the treatment data and help you determine whether it is the bite size that is working (or not), or some other aspect of the treatment. Some intervention teams choose to use standard objects as reference points, such as peas, grains of rice, etc. One helpful tip to consider is that you should use foods that are easy to cut up when implementing size fading, as opposed to foods that are difficult to cut or are too mushy (e.g., canned peaches) or that crumble too easily (e.g., saltine crackers).

### 5.3.1 Advantages

Altering the size of the bite is an easy modification, which often results in increased bite acceptance and consumption. Just like many antecedent modifications, presenting smaller bite sizes, if effective, decreases refusal behaviors because it makes eating easier (or less nonpreferred), so it decreases the motivation to avoid eating.

### 5.3.2 Disadvantages

One disadvantage is the extra time and effort involved in preparing bite sizes and in maintaining consistency of bite sizes across clinicians. Another disadvantage is that it includes extra steps, thus potentially necessitating additional treatment time.

## 5.4 BITE REQUIREMENT/DEMAND FADING

When beginning treatment or introducing a new food, acceptance of nonpreferred foods may be more likely if the feeding task is smaller or easier. One option is to begin intervention with only one or a few bites required per meal, then increasing the bite requirement once the client is consistently consuming bites of nonpreferred foods. For example, on the first day of feeding intervention, Johnny is presented with one bite of each target food: chicken, apple, broccoli, and spaghetti. On day 2, he is presented with two bites of each food; day 3, he is presented with five bites, and so on. There are no black and white rules for how quickly to increase the number of bites per meal. All other things being equal, fading slowly is more likely to be successful but may hold the client back from progressing as fast as he could.

### 5.4.1 Advantages

For escape maintained feeding behaviors, decreasing the motivation to escape will reduce the occurrence of problem behavior to gain escape. Demand fading is a simple variable to manipulate because you are not changing the content or format of the demand, just the amount of demands. It is also a very common sense approach: Just don't make the client eat so much!

### 5.4.2 Disadvantages

Because demand fading involves presenting much smaller meals at first, treatment sessions might not include ample bites of food or variety of foods. Put another way, staff and parents may be highly skeptical of an approach that only requires the client to eat a few bites at first. Of course, very small meals will not provide the client with enough calories. You may need to present a larger number of small meals per day, rather than fewer larger meals. Another option is for the parents to provide the client with an additional meal of preferred foods later that is not considered a treatment meal. If this option is used, be very careful that the additional meal is not presented soon after a treatment meal where the client has failed to eat the prescribed amount of nonpreferred foods. Even for clients with minimal verbal repertoires, it is possible that getting preferred foods soon after refusing nonpreferred foods during treatment meals will reinforce the refusal behavior that occurred during the intervention. Therefore, we often recommend that if parents need to provide supplemental meals outside of treatment meals, they wait at least an hour after a treatment meal if the client had not eaten the expected amount of target nonpreferred foods during the treatment meal.

## 5.5 BLENDING AND SIMULTANEOUS PRESENTATION

Another way to alter the food before presenting it during a feeding session is to present two or more foods at the same time. This is not specific to feeding intervention; simultaneous presentation is a common way for many people to eat foods in daily life (e.g., salad with dressing, carrot with hummus, mashed potatoes with gravy). Typically, preferred foods, or foods that the client has a history of consistently eating (often called *blending agents*), are presented with novel or nonpreferred target foods, or foods that the client does not have a history of eating consistently.

Blending refers to the combination of foods in which they are completely mixed together. Combining nonpreferred foods with preferred foods has been shown to increase consumption of nonpreferred foods (Mueller, Piazza, Patel, Kelley, & Pruett, 2004). Some common ways to do this are to place the target food and the blending agent together in a food processor and blend them, or chop both foods (if in a larger texture) and mix them together, or mix lower texture foods. The ratio of the target food to the blending agent is another variable that can be manipulated. Most often, the blending agent will be presented in a greater ratio to the target food and the blending agent will be thinned out leaving more and more of the target food, as the client is successful. For example, if the target food is broccoli and the blending agent is apple, treatment might start with 90% apple combined with 10% broccoli. Then once the client has met criteria to move forward, the ratio of apple would be decreased as the ratio of broccoli is increased (e.g., 80% apple: 20% broccoli, 70% apple: 30% broccoli, etc.). As the supervisor, you will need to determine individualized criteria for mastery for your client.

### 5.5.1 Advantages

Blending and simultaneous presentation allow you to present target foods during every trial, thus, every trial is a learning opportunity for eating target foods. In addition, for nutrient deficient clients, blending and simultaneous presentation may allow for immediate inclusion of nutrient-dense foods into the diet (if nutrient-dense foods are selected as targets). Also, just as with other discussed antecedent variables, when it works, blending is associated with lower levels of challenging behavior.

## 5.5.2 Disadvantages

Simultaneous presentation and blending require extra planning and preparation time, as well as preparation equipment for blending. Another disadvantage is the potential increased cost since two foods must be provided for each session. In many cases, simultaneous presentation and blending should be considered supplemental supports that should be faded out. For example, it might be fine if the client continues to want to dip french fries in ketchup forever, but it would not be ideal if every bite of vegetables had to be dipped in Ranch dressing forever. A final potential disadvantage is that these approaches can sometimes be disgusting to many others in the client's life (e.g., chocolate sauce on broccoli), so these procedures sometimes have low social validity.

## 5.6 TEXTURE FADING AND CHEWING

Many clients who experience challenges with feeding display texture selectivity, in which they eat only certain textures of food. Often clients with texture selectivity eat mostly softer texture foods, such as baby foods or pureed consistency, rather than age-appropriate table foods. It is also common for clients to eat some regular texture foods, but may display texture selectivity for certain types of foods or preparation (e.g., eats fruits and vegetables only in smoothies or packaged pouches). For clients with texture selectivity such as this, a texture fading procedure in which food texture is gradually faded up may be appropriate.

For clients with texture selectivity, initially reducing the texture of foods will generally increase consumption and decrease escape behavior. Initially, target foods are presented in lower textures and then systematically faded up in texture as the client successfully accepts foods (Najdowski, Tarbox, & Wilke, 2012). Common textures include: puree (baby food), table puree (applesauce consistency), wet ground (oatmeal consistency), ground (ground beef consistency), chopped (chunky salsa consistency), and regular (table foods). An initial probe of various textures can be conducted to find a good starting point. Foods can either be presented one at a time, with repeated presentations, or rotated

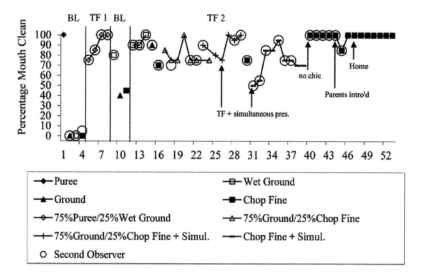

*Figure 5.2 Sample graph of a feeding treatment consisting of escape extinction and texture fading (TF).*
*Note that texture was gradually faded up, parents were introduced into treatment, and meals were generalized to*
*the home setting.* Reprinted from Najdowski, A.C., Tarbox, J., & Wilke, A.E. (2012. Utilizing antecedent
manipulations and reinforcement in the treatment of food selectivity by texture. Education and Treatment of
Children, 35(1), 101–110), with permission from West Virginia University Press.

within each trial set. The clinician presents a predetermined bite size
of the target texture and presents the instruction, "Take a bite."
Reinforcement is provided for the target behavior, if applicable (e.g., bite
acceptance or mouth clean), and inappropriate behaviors are generally
ignored, unless a client-specific behavior intervention is in place during
feeding intervention. The client is given approximately 30 seconds to consume the bite, then the next bite is presented, or the next bite is presented
following the reinforcement interval (Fig. 5.2).

### 5.6.1 Chewing Training

If a client has no history of consuming higher texture foods, the clinician should assess for chewing ability and be aware of the potential for
choking, including being up to date on CPR training. Many children
with severe feeding disorders who are still completely dependent on
baby food have never learned to chew. In these cases, gradual texture
fading as described above may work to increase acceptance of higher
textures. However, in many cases, the client will hold the textured food
in their mouth, without developing the skill to eat it. In such cases, it
is often necessary to directly train the client how to chew. Very little
published research, of which we are aware, has identified the optimal

procedures for teaching chewing skills (Shore, LeBlanc, & Simmons, 1999). However, clinicians have found a variety of procedures to be effective. One approach that can be effective is combining a model prompt (clinician demonstrating vigorously exaggerated and repeated chewing) with a vocal prompt (e.g., "C'mon, chew like a shark, you can do it, chew, chew chew!"). At first, you may need to use additional potent contrived reinforcers just for chewing and then thin them out after chewing skills have become strong and fluent. Another option is to insert a chewy object into the client's mouth when practicing chewing, so that the client receives oral feedback when executing chewing behavior. A good tip to keep in mind is that children who developed typically and were breastfed, babbled, ate baby food, began talking, and gradually had their baby foods increased in texture during the course of development, had many months to develop the skill of chewing. So if your client has never chewed before, do not be surprised if it takes longer than you might have anticipated for you to teach the skill.

### 5.6.2 Advantages
Texture fading is an effective strategy to increase the variety of foods consumed. In addition to being a great way to increase a food repertoire, texture fading also lends well to simultaneous presentation of foods. It is easy to completely combine lower texture foods (e.g., apple sauce with ground chicken), making client separation of those foods more difficult. Perhaps most importantly, texture fading with or without chewing training may be among the only ways that your client is going to learn how to chew and eat textured foods.

### 5.6.3 Disadvantages
Target food textures need to be planned and require extra preparation than regular texture foods. Also, given that texture fading generally involves progressing through various textures before regular texture foods, intervention may take an extended amount of treatment sessions.

## 5.7 NONCONTINGENT REINFORCEMENT

Noncontingent reinforcement (NCR) is an antecedent intervention in which the client receives the reinforcer independent of their behavior. Reinforcement is delivered continuously or on a fixed or variable time schedule. NCR is used to decrease the client's motivation to engage in problem behavior. In the case of feeding, NCR is used to make the overall feeding scenario less nonpreferred, thereby decreasing the value of escape from eating as a reinforcer for refusal behaviors (Reed et al., 2004). A simple and common way to use NCR is to provide continuous access to a preferred object or activity. For example, the client can play a game on his iPad, watch TV, or play with his favorite car while bites are presented. Breaks can also be presented as NCR, which may be effective in reducing escape maintained problem behavior within feeding, but transitioning back to the feeding environment should be a consideration (if breaks are taken away from the table). When using fixed or variable time schedules of NCR, the schedule can be determined by using the average interresponse time (IRT) of problem behavior, then delivering reinforcement before the average occurrence of problem behavior would occur. For example, if the client engaged in tantrums every 5 minutes, reinforcement can be delivered every 4 minutes, independent of any behavior occurring at that time (i.e., noncontingent).

## 5.7.1 Advantages

There are many advantages to using NCR. First, it is easy to administer. The clinician does not need to monitor behavioral contingencies since reinforcement is delivered based on time or on a continuous schedule. In addition, although the published literature on NCR for feeding is not yet extensive, NCR has much empirical support for reducing problem behavior and avoiding extinction bursts in general.

## 5.7.2 Disadvantages

Due to the lack of a reinforcement contingency, NCR might inadvertently reinforce problem behavior if the planned time of delivery happens to immediately follow challenging behavior. As such, it is common practice to wait a short period (e.g., 5 s) after the occurrence of problem behavior before delivering reinforcement. Also, it is sometimes desirable to thin the reinforcement schedule to contingencies more similar to the natural environment. For example, if Joey is allowed to continuously watch TV when learning to eat new foods (NCR), intervention might eventually move to Joey earning a TV show when he is done with dinner (DRA).

## 5.8 HIGH-P/LOW-P SEQUENCE

The high-p/low-p sequence, sometimes referred to as "behavioral momentum," has been demonstrated to effectively increase the acceptance of nonpreferred foods (Penrod, Gardella, & Fernand, 2012). This intervention includes presenting several instructions that have a history of compliance (e.g., easier instructions) immediately before a target instruction that does not have a history of compliance (e.g., difficult instruction). For feeding, this can be done in a variety of ways. One is to present several bites of preferred foods in a row, followed by a bite of a nonpreferred food (e.g., bite of apple, bite of apple, bite of apple, bite of broccoli). Bite size can also be used to create high-p/low-p sequence (e.g., pea-sized bite, pea-sized bite, dime-sized bite), as well as texture (e.g., pureed bite, pureed bite, pureed bite, regular bite). Any type of bite that has a history of being consistently consumed can be presented several times in a row, then followed by a bite that the client does not yet consistently eat.

### 5.8.1 Advantages

Similar to other antecedent interventions, the high-p/low-p sequence can help to reduce problem behaviors. In addition, the presentation of high-p instructions allows for many opportunities for the maintenance of mastered foods. This request sequence is fairly easy to implement and may be a good choice for caregiver implementation.

### 5.8.2 Disadvantages

A prerequisite for this intervention is that the client has several mastered foods to use on high-p requests. Another disadvantage is that, because the nonpreferred food is embedded within several high-p instructions, there are fewer learning opportunities for the nonpreferred foods. Finally, this procedure usually is not effective alone; it often requires the addition of escape extinction.

# CHAPTER 6

# Common Treatment Packages

In this chapter, we describe how to implement treatment packages for feeding disorders. Treatment packages are practical, real-life behavioral interventions that combine different procedural components (e.g., differential reinforcement of alternative behavior plus nonremoval of the spoon) and are generally effective because of multiple different behavioral principles (e.g., motivating operations, positive reinforcement, and extinction; not just one). You may be wondering which of the treatment packages in this chapter are the best or most effective, but as with every other specialty within applied behavior analysis (ABA), there is no best option that applies across all clients. The treatment packages that we chose to include in this chapter are those with the most research support, those that are most commonly used in feeding treatment centers of excellence, and a few that we included because we have had especially good success with them in our practice. The process of selection between different treatment components to design your initial treatment package, implementation, and then customization to optimize effectiveness is described in Chapters 7 and 9.

## 6.1 STIMULUS FADING PLUS DIFFERENTIAL REINFORCEMENT OF ALTERNATIVE BEHAVIOR

Combining stimulus fading and differential reinforcement of alternative behavior (DRA) can be an effective intervention, or at the very least, a useful way to begin an intervention. The combination of these procedures into a treatment package has been demonstrated to increase food consumption (Freeman & Piazza, 1998). The rationale for this combination of treatment components is that, if stimulus fading is done well and if very powerful positive reinforcers are presented for consumption, you may not need to use escape extinction. For this reason, if the team has enough time to try out a variety of treatment options and parameters (i.e., it is not absolutely urgent that the client's eating improves

Treating Feeding Challenges in Autism. DOI: http://dx.doi.org/10.1016/B978-0-12-813563-1.00006-9

immediately), we highly recommend that you try to make this treatment package work first, before resorting to escape extinction.

To implement stimulus fading plus DRA, present a very small bite of nonpreferred food and give the client a very powerful reinforcer contingent on acceptance of the bite (see descriptions of bite sizes and size fading in Chapters 3 and 5). For example, if the client eats an eighth of a bite of spinach, then you give him a bite of chicken nugget. If the client refuses the bite of nonpreferred food, remove it for 30 seconds and then present another bite. If this procedure is effective, gradually increase the size of the bites over successive meals, until the terminal bite size is reached. If this procedure is not effective, consider increasing the magnitude of the positive reinforcer. For example, if the client eats an eighth of a bite of spinach, give him two, three, or five bites of chicken nugget. It may seem ridiculous to give the client such a large amount of preferred food for eating such a small amount of nonpreferred food, but if it works without escape extinction, it may be worth it. Over successive successful meals, gradually increase the bite size and decrease the amount of positive reinforcement. If increasing the size of the reinforcer does not work, consider trying a much more potent reinforcer (e.g., ice cream).

Naturally, if you want a positive reinforcer to work, it is important to ensure that the client does not have free access to it outside of treatment meals. If possible, completely restrict access to that particular positive reinforcer outside of treatment meals. If you are having a difficult time identifying a positive reinforcer that is powerful enough and your client has a particularly strong interest (e.g., obsessed with trains, a particular video, etc.), consider using access to that interest as the positive reinforcer for eating. You may be concerned about encouraging the client to engage in the interest by using it as a reinforcer, but it may be worth it to do it in the short term if it works to increase food consumption. You can always fade that out of the treatment later, after the client has developed a healthy and varied eating repertoire.

### 6.1.1 Advantages
One advantage to this treatment package is that it does not include escape extinction, so potential side effects of that procedure are avoided. This combination of an antecedent manipulation and positive reinforcement will likely avoid producing an increase in challenging behaviors while still teaching appropriate feeding behaviors.

## 6.1.2 Disadvantages

Given that the terminal/goal bite is being modified, stimulus fading involves multiple steps, requiring management and potentially requiring additional time. Another disadvantage to this treatment package is that it often does not work, since you are intentionally letting the client escape from eating for 30 seconds each time they refuse a bite. Some clients will therefore continue to refuse every bite and never eat the nonpreferred foods.

## 6.2 DIFFERENTIAL REINFORCEMENT OF ALTERNATIVE BEHAVIOR PLUS ESCAPE EXTINCTION

Unfortunately, research has shown that positive reinforcement alone is often insufficient to increase consumption (Piazza, Patel, Gulotta, Sevin, & Layer, 2003); therefore, escape extinction and DRA are often combined. If you have already unsuccessfully tried decreasing bite size and increasing the magnitude of positive reinforcement, it may be warranted to try escape extinction. This treatment package has been very well established in the literature for effectively treating feeding problems (Piazza et al., 2003). In this treatment, positive reinforcement is presented for the target eating response (e.g., acceptance or mouth clean) and any inappropriate behavior no longer produces escape. Head turns, bats, or any other refusal behaviors are ignored and the bite remains present/is presented again until consumed. For example, Hugo is presented with a bite of broccoli. If he accepts the bite into his mouth, he is given 1 minute access to an iPad. However, if he refuses the broccoli, the bite remains in front of him until he consumes it. See more detail on escape extinction in Chapter 4, Treatment Components: Positive Reinforcement and Escape Extinction, including procedural variations.

## 6.2.1 Advantages

This treatment package has a great amount of research support. Additionally, differential reinforcement of alternative behavior plus escape extinction does not require any extra treatment steps or special food preparation.

## 6.2.2 Disadvantages

Just as with other packaged treatments containing escape extinction, there is the potential for unwanted side effects, including the fact that parents and the client may find it nonpreferred. Another variable that is worth considering is the fact that most research that has shown that

DRA alone does not work (and they therefore add escape extinction) made little or no attempt to modify positive reinforcement to make it more effective; e.g., increasing the magnitude, duration, or variety of positive reinforcers. In addition, few such studies systematically attempted to vary antecedent components before resorting to escape extinction; e.g., decreasing bite size, etc. For these reasons, we strongly recommend you give a wholehearted effort at optimizing the effectiveness of positive reinforcement for eating before adding escape extinction.

## 6.3 DIFFERENTIAL REINFORCEMENT OF ALTERNATIVE BEHAVIOR PLUS REINFORCEMENT THINNING PLUS DEMAND FADING PLUS ESCAPE EXTINCTION

This treatment package has an unreasonably long name because it contains many treatment components. However, it is actually quite simple from a procedural standpoint and research has shown that it can be effective (Najdowski, Wallace, Doney, & Ghezzi, 2003). To illustrate the procedure, imagine that the very first treatment meal involves the client having to eat one-eighth of one bite of nonpreferred foods in order to receive a whole plate of dessert. In the final meal of the procedure, the client needs to eat a regularly sized, nutritionally balanced meal, in order to earn a reasonably sized dessert. All of the meals that take place between the first and the last one involve gradually increasing the size and number of bites required before dessert is given, while also gradually decreasing the size of the dessert from a whole plate to one reasonable portion. In addition, some variation of escape extinction may also be needed, but you can try implementing all of the other components first. The number of different steps that you plan between the first meal and the last depends on how fast you want to fade the treatment. Generally speaking, fading more quickly can produce faster results but is more likely to fail, whereas fading more slowly may take longer but is more likely to succeed.

| Step Number | 1 | 2 | 3 | 4 | 5 | 6 | 7 | 8 | 9 | 10 |
|---|---|---|---|---|---|---|---|---|---|---|
| Nonpref. foods amount | 1 bite | 2 bites | 3 bites | 5 bites | 8 bites | 12 bites | 18 bites | 27 bites | 41 bites | 62 bites |
| Dessert size | Whole plate | Whole plate | Whole plate | 3/4 plate | 1/2 plate | Double portion | 1.75 portions | 1.5 portions | 1.25 portion | 1 portion |

### 6.3.1 Advantages

An advantage of this procedure is that it is simple to understand and manage procedurally: First, the client receives a huge amount of reinforcement for eating nonpreferred foods, and then, it is gradually thinned, until reaching a typical meal.

### 6.3.2 Disadvantages

A disadvantage of this procedure is that there are multiple steps to plan and manage. However, the progression of the steps is logical and the minute details of the progression likely are not overly critical. Another disadvantage of the procedure is that it involves giving the client an unreasonable amount of dessert for the first few meals. Many parents may be hesitant to allow the client to eat such a large amount of unhealthy foods in the beginning. An alternative is to present a large amount of some other very highly preferred foods, not dessert. As long as they are a potent reinforcer, that option may work equally well. A final disadvantage is that the procedure is not applicable to clients who do not already have highly preferred foods at the outset of treatment, but this same disadvantage is shared by all treatment packages that use preferred food as positive reinforcement.

## 6.4 NONCONTINGENT REINFORCEMENT PLUS ESCAPE EXTINCTION

Combining noncontingent reinforcement with escape extinction can be an effective treatment package that is also likely to be preferred by clients and parents (Reed et al., 2004). To implement this treatment package, provide continuous access to preferred toys/videos/activities and attention throughout the meal, in addition to escape extinction for refusal behaviors. NCR may consist of the client playing with items or watching a video while the clinician praises, sings songs, etc. Reinforcement remains in place and bites of target foods are presented approximately every 30 seconds. Escape extinction is implemented for challenging behavior (e.g., nonremoval of the spoon or nonremoval of the meal) (Fig. 6.1).

### 6.4.1 Advantages

Just like any implementation of noncontingent reinforcement, this component of the treatment is easy for clinicians and caregivers to implement and is preferred by the client. NCR may also reduce the

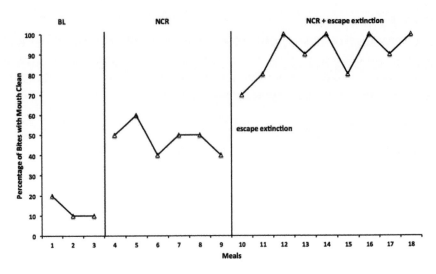

*Figure 6.1 Sample graph of noncontingent reinforcement (NCR) producing significant but inadequate improvements in consumption. In this hypothetical case, adding escape extinction was necessary to effectively improve consumption of nonpreferred foods.*

aversiveness of mealtime, thus preventing challenging behaviors. NCR is rarely, if ever, effective alone, so adding escape extinction produces a treatment package that is highly likely to both preferred by the client and effective.

### 6.4.2 Disadvantages

Including the escape extinction component of this treatment package increases the possibility of the negative side effects of extinction, such as bursting and emotional responses, and may therefore be nonpreferred by parents and clients.

### 6.5 NONCONTINGENT REINFORCEMENT PLUS NONEXCLUSIONARY TIMEOUT

Combining noncontingent reinforcement with a nonexclusionary time-out is a treatment package that can be very easy for clinicians and caregivers to implement because, although it is complicated from a conceptual standpoint, the procedure is very straightforward. At the beginning of the meal, the client is given a highly preferred reinforcer for free at the beginning of the meal and they keep it as long as they continue to eat bites when the bites are presented to them. If at any

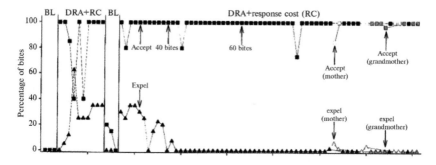

*Figure 6.2 Sample graph of a feeding treatment consisting of noncontingent reinforcement plus nonexclusionary timeout (referred to as DRA + response cost on the graph). Note that meal size was gradually increased to 60 bites and the client's mother and grandmother were trained to implement treatment.* Reprinted from Kahng, S., Tarbox, J., & Wilke, A.E. (2001). Use of a multicomponent treatment for food refusal. Journal of Applied Behavior Analysis, 34(1), 93–96, with permission from Wiley.

point the client refuses a bite, the clinician removes the reinforcer. The client can only get the reinforcer back by taking another bite, at which point the clinician gives the reinforcer back and the client keeps it until she refuses a bite again in the future or until she has consumed the entire meal. It is important to note that the term "nonexclusionary timeout" in the name of the procedure does NOT imply that you are placing the client in seclusion in any way. It simply means that you are removing access to positive reinforcers temporarily. The client remains in the same place for the entire meal, regardless of whether they eat, hence the word "nonexclusionary" in the name.

When choosing what positive reinforcers to use, select ones that are prolonged in duration and that the client will want to keep for the entire meal. For example, watching videos or playing simple games on a computer tablet. It is wise to avoid foods as the positive reinforcer in this procedure because the client would need to be given continuous access to the preferred foods throughout the meal, which would likely result in her satiating on that food rapidly.

Fig. 6.2 is reproduced from Kahng, Tarbox, and Wilke (2001), the first study to include this procedure. Originally, it was referred to as "DRA plus response cost." However, we think the procedure is better described as noncontingent reinforcement plus timeout, because the reinforcers are given for free at the beginning of the meal. There are likely several behavioral principles that make the procedure work. First, NCR likely makes the meal less aversive and therefore is an abolishing operation for escape as a reinforcer. Second, when the clinician removes reinforcement contingent on refusal behavior, that consequence likely punishes the behavior (i.e., the contingent removal of a positively reinforcing stimulus). Third, since continuing to eat prevents removal of the positive reinforcer, eating is negatively reinforced through avoidance of reinforcer removal. Finally, once the reinforcers are gone, they can only be regained by eating; therefore, the delivery of reinforcers contingent on eating likely positively reinforces eating.

### 6.5.1 Advantages

A major advantage of this procedure is that it is simple to train parents and staff on. Another advantage is that it can be highly preferred by the client because they get to engage in a highly preferred activity for the entire meal, so long as they continue to eat. A further advantage is that it can work without escape extinction.

### 6.5.2 Disadvantages

A disadvantage of the procedure is that it includes removing positive reinforcement, which is a form of punishment. However, this is a least intrusive form of punishment and toy removal is something that parents already do on a regular basis when a child misbehaves. We almost always start with positive reinforcement for eating or noncontingent reinforcement before adding a nonexclusionary timeout component.

# CHAPTER 7

# Treatment Management

Feeding treatment programs require expert supervision and management, just like any other behavioral intervention program for individuals with autism spectrum disorder (ASD). In this chapter, we provide practical guidance regarding qualifications and training for staff, describe the various models of treatment management and supervision that you can use in the context of feeding treatment, and give guidelines for the data collection and treatment-evaluation process.

## 7.1 STAFFING

Generally speaking, implementing behavioral intervention for feeding disorders is a technical process that should be done by professionals who have had substantial training by masters or PhD-level experts in feeding intervention. A few parent-mediated models have been effective (and are discussed briefly below), but feeding intervention generally requires at least two levels of professional staffing; the therapists working directly with the client and the behavior analysts that supervise them.

### 7.1.1 Therapists

We will refer to the clinician who works directly with the client and presents the meals as the "therapist." We chose this term because it is probably the most commonly used term in the applied behavior analysis (ABA) community to refer to the high school or bachelor- level clinician who works directly with clients and it is not to be confused with what "therapist" means in general psychology (i.e., psychotherapist). Other common terms for the behavioral clinician who works directly with the client include "technician," "tutor," "instructor," and "interventionist." The therapist in a feeding program must have rigorous training in behavioral principles and procedures, as all feeding treatments are derived from those basic principles and procedures. Ideally, therapists should be Registered Behavioral Technicians™ (RBT®) and/

Treating Feeding Challenges in Autism. DOI: http://dx.doi.org/10.1016/B978-0-12-813563-1.00007-0

or possess approximately 40 hours of didactic and hands-on training in the general principles and procedures of ABA, as well as the specific treatment procedures described in this book. Therapists should also be trained on CPR and behavioral emergency measures, such as crisis prevention intervention.

### 7.1.1.1 Parents as Therapists

Research has shown that parents can effectively serve as therapists in feeding interventions, just as they can be effectively trained to implement other nonfeeding-related behavioral interventions with their children. However, like with any behavioral intervention procedure, if parents are to serve as therapists for their child's feeding interventions, they must be trained and supervised properly. Behavioral skills training (BST) should be used to train parents to proficiency before they are asked to implement the procedures with their child. BST consists of the following three steps:

1. **Describe** the procedures, including the rationale and how to implement them. You should also provide a written protocol description, composed in lay language that is easy to understand (i.e., avoid unnecessary technical jargon). Depending on how complicated the feeding treatment procedures are and how much prior experience the parent has, this step could take as little as 10 minutes or as much as an hour or two. Continue this step until the parent can explain the procedure back to you and has no more questions for you.
2. **Model** the procedures by demonstrating exactly how you would actually implement them, including all of the materials, and ideally in the actual location in which the parent is to implement it later (e.g., kitchen table). Continue modeling until the procedure has been clearly demonstrated and the parent has no more questions.
3. **Role-play** the procedures with the parent and give live-ongoing feedback. First, the parent should take the role of the child and the trainer takes the role of the parent feeding the "child." Make sure the parent role-plays all possible behaviors the child might display during all phases of the treatment. Then, switch roles and the trainer plays the role of the child and the parent plays the role of her/himself. Again, make sure to act out all possible behaviors the child is likely to display. Throughout the role-playing process, give immediate, frank, and upbeat feedback to the parent on their implementation. Try to make it lighthearted and fun, while being

respectful of the possibility that feeding challenges may be a source of genuine stress for the parent. Continue role-playing until the parent demonstrates excellent performance. Consider collecting data on the accuracy of the parent's implementation and continuing role-play until accuracy is at 90% or higher.

After role-play is complete, make sure that the behavior analyst who is supervising the case directly observes the parent to implement many meals, in order to ensure she/he is doing so accurately. The supervisor should continue to supervise meals as much or more than if a professional therapist was implementing them (supervision is discussed further below).

### 7.1.1.1.1 Strengths

Several advantages to having parents serve as the therapists are worth noting. First, it requires far less time on the part of professionals, as professionals are not actually delivering the vast majority of hours of treatment. This may result in less overhead and less logistical challenges for behavior analysts, potentially resulting in clinicians being able to serve more families or serve families in regions where professional entry-level staff may be hard to recruit. Second, and more importantly, when parents serve as the therapists, they are intimately involved in the behavior-change process from the very start. When supervised effectively, this results in parents having intensive direct experience with the power of behavior-change procedures to make a real difference in their child's life. Parents are thus learning *to do* behavioral intervention, not just learning about it.

### 7.1.1.1.2 Limitations

Several limitations of having parents serve as therapists are worth noting. First, if parents serve as therapists from the very beginning, they will likely experience the most difficult phase of treatment, including initial extinction bursts and treatment refinement and adjustment. Second, the emotional intensity of treating their own child's severe behavior can be a major challenge for many parents and may not be surmountable for some parents. Third, in some sense, parents should not have to treat their own child's feeding disorder. That is why professionals exist, so that parents are not burdened with this responsibility. Parents are not expected to be their own child's teacher, speech therapist, or medical doctor, so they should not be expected to be their child's feeding therapist either.

## 7.1.2 Supervisors

Supervisors should be either masters or PhD-level behavior analysts and should possess either the Board Certified Behavior Analyst (BCBA) or BCBA-Doctoral certifications. In addition to these minimum credentials, supervisors must possess specialized training and experience in the treatment of feeding disorders. Unfortunately, most behavior analysts have not had adequate training and experience in treating feeding disorders and, indeed, that fact was part of the impetus for writing this book. Even after reading this book and/or relevant journal articles, behavior analysts should seek out mentorship from other behavior analysts who are already experts in treating feeding disorders before considering themselves qualified to supervise feeding treatment without supervision from someone else more experienced. Of course, the same is true for other specializations within ABA. Someone who only has experience in functional analysis and treatment of severe self-injurious behavior is not qualified to supervise intensive skill acquisition programs for young children with autism, and someone who has only done the latter is similarly not qualified to supervise the former. So if you are reading this book and you have not actually done any of the procedures described in this book before, we highly recommend you to hire a behavior analyst who specializes in feeding disorders to consult with you as your mentor. You should continue to retain their mentorship and gradually fade out their oversight as you gradually demonstrate competence at supervising feeding intervention yourself.

## 7.2 MANAGEMENT MODELS

Behavioral interventions for feeding disorders must be supervised with at least the same level of intensity and rigor as other behavioral interventions. There is no black and white rule about how much time a feeding program must be supervised, but a good rule of thumb is to follow the Behavior Analyst Certification Board (BACB) recommendations for supervising-focused treatment programs for children with autism, which states that approximately 2 hours of supervision should be spent for every 10 hours of direct treatment (BACB, 2014). The supervisor's job is to monitor ongoing progress and use the principles of behavior to customize and troubleshoot the treatment program and we discuss supervision models below.

## 7.2.1 Direct Supervision

The majority of supervision should be in-vivo, face-to-face supervision provided by a BCBA who is physically present to observe the therapists implement meals. This supervision should then also be backed up by occasional meetings outside of meals, where the supervisor and therapists have the opportunity to review data together, discuss progress, plan the next several meals, and troubleshoot where necessary. These supervision interactions can occur in the context of a variety of formats, which we discuss below.

### 7.2.1.1 Within a Comprehensive ABA Program

This supervision model includes providing feeding intervention as a component of the client's comprehensive ABA program. If the BCBA who is already supervising the client's overall ABA program is competent to supervise feeding treatment, then they can simply add a feeding program to the overall treatment program. For example, a client might have feeding as part of his session each day (e.g., lunch time) or during each session if multiple ABA sessions occur each day. Just like all other programs within the client's overall treatment plan, the intensity of the feeding program will depend on the client's individual needs and overall treatment intensity and schedule. Occasionally, it is useful to put most of the other programs in the client's overall treatment plan on hold for a few weeks, so you can spend the majority of treatment time to intensively focus on feeding until an effective intervention is identified.

### 7.2.1.2 Direct Consultation

Supervision of a feeding program can also be provided as an independent service. Treatment management using this model includes directly assessing, planning treatment, and overseeing feeding intervention outside or separate from a comprehensive ABA program. Typically, this type of treatment model is utilized when a different provider is implementing a comprehensive ABA program, and a BCBA specializing in feeding treatment solely provides feeding treatment. Moreover, if a client is not receiving any ABA intervention, a BCBA may be brought in to treat feeding problems only.

### 7.2.1.3 School Consultation

School-age children spend the majority of their day in school and therefore healthy eating in schools is important to ensure they are accessing necessary nutrition to contribute to their overall health, as well as success in the school setting. A BCBA supervisor can work with the teacher, paraprofessional (if applicable), and other members of the individualized education plan (IEP) team to assess feeding difficulties or mealtime challenging behaviors, develop treatment goals, and implement feeding intervention in the school environment. Such treatment settings can range from 1:1 eating, to small groups, to eating with the whole class or larger group during school mealtimes. The supervisor might provide school consultation to treat feeding problems for students as an employee on an internal consultation model, or as an outside consultant. Furthermore, school consultation may be the primary context for feeding intervention or may be a goal for generalization as part of a broader feeding intervention that primarily took place outside of school. Regardless, there are many challenges inherent in school consultation and space does not permit a thorough discussion here. Among the most important points to consider is the fact that you, as a consultant, generally do not possess the authority to compel any of the school staff to do what you recommend, as you would if they were your direct employees. It is therefore critical to focus on building collaborative relationships, based on mutual support and respect.

### 7.2.2 Telemedicine

Unfortunately, there simply aren't enough behavior analysts with specific training to supervise behavioral feeding intervention directly. Very few experts in feeding disorders are available to provide treatment and the number of clients in need of the service far exceeds the number of clinicians trained to provide treatment (Clawson et al., 2008). Further, the cost and/or logistics required to travel to a feeding clinic may not be a realistic option for many individuals in need.

An alternate method of supervision is telemedicine. This avenue of treatment provides treatment via electronic communications (e.g., two-way video, email, smart phones, and other technology). Generally, a BCBA trained in feeding intervention provides assessment and treatment planning for the client by use of some form of video conference. For example, the supervisor provides supervision appointments via Skype, which allows her to observe feeding sessions in real time. Telemedicine can be utilized to coach caregivers or on-site clinicians to provide direct feeding intervention. All of the same variables that affect in-person supervision are relevant and other variables make the process even more challenging. For example, problems inevitably arise with the technology being used and even with live video conference, all parties may have difficulty in hearing and seeing one another adequately to allow for effective supervision in the same amount of time one might normally dedicate to supervision. BST, including instructions, modeling, rehearsal, and feedback should still be provided to train caregivers and on-site clinicians, just as you would do in-person.

### 7.2.2.1 Advantages

Telemedicine is an established model of treatment in the medical field that may help give access to many people in need of treatment. If done effectively, telemedicine should allow for dissemination of evidence-based feeding intervention around the world.

### 7.2.2.2 Disadvantages

Currently, there is little research to specifically support the use of telemedicine to treat feeding problems. However, research has shown that telemedicine can be used to successfully train parents to treat problem behavior (Wacker et al., 2013). Another potential disadvantage is that some popular video conferencing softwares, such as Skype, are not compliant with the Health Insurance Portability and Accountability Act, so make sure to thoroughly investigate the best software to use before using it.

## 7.3 CHOOSING TREATMENT COMPONENTS AND INITIAL TREATMENT DESIGN

The process of initially designing your treatment package before first implementing it is complex and there are many difficult decisions to be made. Unfortunately, many clinicians neglect to consider many of these decisions and instead simply repeat what they or their mentors normally do. Instead, we recommend carefully weighing all variables you are aware of and engaging the client's parents and/or other stakeholders in frank discussion about the various options. We also highly recommend you consult the BACB *Professional and Ethical Compliance Code for Behavior Analysts* (Behavior Analyst Certification Board, 2016) on a regular basis while designing and supervising feeding treatment. Below, we provide some brief points to consider. Keep in mind, these are NOT the rules to follow, they are merely some of the points we recommend you to consider while making your own decisions, given all of the unique variables impacting each individual case.

- **Use Positive Reinforcement.** If there is any general rule that *almost always* applies, it is this. Even if you think it will have no impact at all, it is an ethical imperative to always at least try to give the client some kind of positive reinforcement as a consequence for eating nonpreferred foods (i.e., differential reinforcement of alternative behavior (DRA)) or noncontingently (i.e., noncontingent reinforcement (NCR)).
- **If it is not an emergency, try varying parameters of reinforcement, bite size, and others, before using escape extinction.** If you have time, it is usually the most ethical choice to exhaust many other options before implementing escape extinction. Fig. 7.1 is a flowchart that

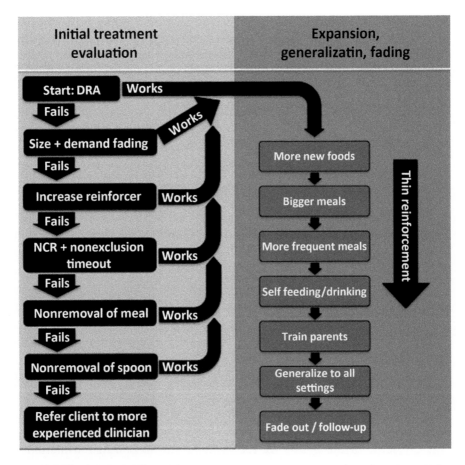

*Figure 7.1 Example of one possible progression through evaluating initial treatment components and then expanding treatment, fading it out, and training parents.*

depicts one possible sequence of intervention components to try, generally progressing from less-to-more intrusive. You can add treatment components in this progression or you can replace the previous treatment with the next one. Generally speaking, adding components makes the treatment more likely to be effective but also more complex and more difficult to manage. The progression in this flowchart assumes you have a reasonable amount of time to try a variety of procedures that might not work, which is not always the case. The best progression will be different for every client and must be determined by the BCBA, in collaboration with the parents and client.

- **Nonremoval of the spoon is probably the fastest and most likely to be an effective procedure.** At the time this book is being written, no other treatment procedure had the same level of research support nor the decades of proven effectiveness in clinical practice as nonremoval of the spoon. It almost always works, and it works quickly.
- **Intervene as intensively as possible.** A common pitfall within most comprehensive ABA programs is to address feeding infrequently and to dedicate inadequate time to it. If it is at all possible, temporarily make feeding the primary focus of the client's overall ABA program and ensure as many feeding learning opportunities as possible. Implement feeding treatment meals every day, even multiple times per day, if it can be done with high treatment integrity.
- **Focus on parent and client preference.** In technical behavioral terms, always take into account the social validity of treatment procedures. Involve the parents and client in all phases of treatment design, choice, and adjustment/modification. Whenever it is possible to do so effectively, do the procedures that parents and clients want you to do. If you ever have two treatments of equal effectiveness, allow the client to choose.

Whatever treatment you choose to implement at first, it is very rare for it to work perfectly the first time. Treatment management and evaluation is a gradual, iterative process.

## 7.4 TREATMENT EVALUATION VIA GRAPHING AND DATA ANALYSIS

In order to determine the effectiveness of your feeding intervention, you will need to analyze the data on a daily basis. As with all behavioral interventions, graphing and visually inspecting data are cornerstones of the treatment process. Data should be graphed after every meal and should be visually inspected by the supervisor frequently and before any major treatment phase or treatment adjustment is made.

### 7.4.1 Visual Analysis

When visually inspecting a graph, evaluate these primary aspects of the data:

1. **Level.** The extent to which the level of the behavior changes in the desired direction. Effective feeding interventions increase consumption and decrease challenging behaviors to a large degree and do so relatively quickly (changes in level are usually seen within only a few meals).
2. **Trend.** The extent to which three or more successive meals of data are going in the same direction, either up or down. Effective feeding interventions produce upward trends in consumption and downward trends in challenging behavior.
3. **Variability.** The amount of "bounce" in the data. The amount of separation between the highest highs and lowest lows within the same phase. All other things being equal, more variability makes data harder to read. Effective feeding interventions generally reduce the overall amount of variability in the data, with consumption being near 100% and remaining high. Some amount of variability is natural, even with very effective interventions, but not so much that it represents a clinically significant problem with mealtimes.

Visual analysis of multiple data points on a graph is different from traditional statistics; in that the purpose is to identify treatments that have strong effects, not merely statistically significant effects. Feeding treatments can be particularly effective, so look for substantial upward trends in the feeding behaviors you are trying to increase and expect the client's eating to improve so that the client is consistently consuming 80% or more of the food presented to her. We discuss data analysis further when we describe experimental designs below.

### 7.4.2 Experimental Designs

This book is for practitioners, not researchers, and therefore, we are not going to dedicate a large amount of space to discussing experimental designs. However, ABA is a very unique discipline in that we use research designs every day to evaluate the effectiveness of our clinical practice. Below, we describe how single-case experimental designs that were developed for research in ABA can be customized for practical evaluation of treatment in real-life settings.

### 7.4.2.1 AB Design

The AB design is the simplest way to evaluate the effectiveness of a treatment. It is almost never rigorous enough to be published in a peer-reviewed scientific journal but is often good enough for evaluating real-life treatment (Kazdin, 2011). Fig. 7.2 is a sample AB design graph of feeding intervention. To evaluate your feeding intervention with an AB design, you first conduct a baseline phase.

7.4.2.1.1 Baseline
It is important to conduct baseline meals before beginning a new feeding intervention, in order to assess how effective the intervention really is. There are several options for how to run baseline meals but most options can be roughly categorized as either *natural baselines* or *analog baselines*. Natural baseline meals are just what they sound like: Normal meals that the caregiver or clinician used to present, before a new intervention plan was designed. Some amount of structure or guidance can be given during natural baseline meals, such as

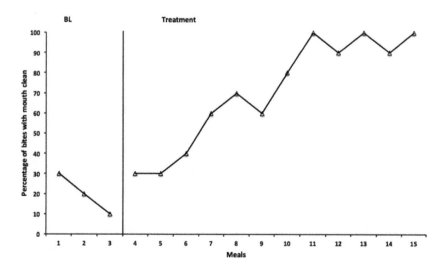

*Figure 7.2 Sample graph of an AB design, consisting of baseline and a successful treatment.*

the types of foods to include and the approximate number of bites and/or amount of food to be presented. To conduct a truly natural baseline meal, you would not change the contingencies for the client's behavior. For example, if the parent was implementing the meal, you might tell the parent, "Just do what you normally would do, if I wasn't here." An advantage of natural baseline meals is that staff and caregivers are allowed to just do what is already natural to them. A disadvantage is that, as they are much less controlled, unexpected, uncontrolled variables can make the client's feeding appear more or less problematic than it might be under more consistently controlled conditions.

Analog baseline meals have structured contingencies that are analogous to what you believe the problematic reinforcement contingencies were in the client's natural life. For example, you might intentionally give 30 seconds of escape from nonpreferred food as a consequence of each occurrence of food refusal behavior. An advantage of analog baseline meals is that they allow you to give clear structure and directions to the person presenting the meal (which may be preferred by parents and staff) and they allow you to carefully control the contingencies so you can more accurately identify what really works when changing from baseline to treatment. Disadvantages of analog baseline meals is that they may appear artificial to parents and staff (because they *are* artificially arranged) and that they often involve intentionally reinforcing refusal behavior with escape from eating. However, analog baseline meals are by far the more commonly used option in published research and dozens of studies have shown very effective treatment following analog baselines, so reinforcing refusal behavior with escape during baseline does not appear to harm the effectiveness of intervention.

However you choose to format baseline, if the team reasonably does not know how much of a particular target food the client will eat and how much challenging behavior she is likely to engage in, multiple baseline meals may be necessary. If the client's caregivers and entire team are completely sure the client has always refused the particular foods that are to be targeted, a single baseline meal confirming this may be sufficient. If the first meal or two produces highly variable patterns of eating, you may need to conduct more baseline meals in order to observe a stable baseline phase.

### 7.4.2.1.2 Treatment Phase

After a stable baseline has been established, a phase line should be drawn on the graph and the first meal of the intervention phase is conducted. The new treatment should be implemented for a sufficient number of meals so that any change in level, trend, and variability, relative to baseline, can be evaluated. Most published feeding research (and our clinical experience) has demonstrated that effective feeding interventions generally produce relatively stable consumption of non-preferred foods that is close to 100%. Some treatments work more rapidly than others but, if the treatment is going to work, you should start to see an increasing trend in the target behavior within a few meals. Very often, you will see an extinction burst (temporary increase in rate and intensity of challenging behavior) in the first meal. Although extinction bursts can be difficult to manage, as long as you are able to follow-through with extinction, bursts are actually a good sign that the treatment is working.

There is no black and white rule for how fast a treatment should work, but if your treatment does not produce and sustain a clear upward trend within a few meals (perhaps 3–7), you may want to consider modifying the treatment to enhance its effectiveness. But do not be tempted to change the treatment too rapidly, given a single particularly successful or unsuccessful meal. If and when you implement each significant change in the treatment package, draw a phase line on the graph so you can more easily evaluate whether the change increased effectiveness. For smaller changes or "tweaks" to the intervention plan, many clinicians prefer to draw an arrow that indicates on the graph where the change was made, rather than drawing a phase line. Similarly, as the client meets milestones in the treatment process (new foods introduced, bite size increased, bites per meal increased, switching to self-feeding, etc.), phase lines or arrows should be added to the graph to mark the changes.

### 7.4.2.2 Reversal Design

AB designs suffer from a fatal flaw: You can never really know for sure whether it was the treatment that produced the behavior change or whether it is possible that something else happened around the same time that influenced the behavior. This is why AB designs are inadequate for research. In everyday treatment, the plausibility that some other variable just happened to fix the problem right at the

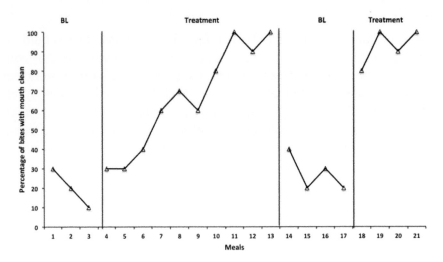

*Figure 7.3 Sample graph of an ABAB design, consisting of baseline, successful treatment, reversal to baseline, and final reversal back to treatment. ABAB designs can be very effective in demonstrating a cause-and-effect relationship between the treatment and the effect it has on improving feeding.*

same time that you started intervention is low enough that AB designs are usually adequate. However, there are occasional situations in clinical practice when the evidence produced by an AB design is honestly not enough to meet your needs. For example, if a medication is changed at the same time, the client became ill or got over an illness, or a major change in client staffing or nonfeeding-related behavioral intervention occurred at the same time that the feeding intervention was started. Another situation in which an AB may be inadequate is if other important stakeholders (e.g., parents, teachers, funding agencies) do not believe the treatment was responsible for the improvement in feeding and it is important to convince them. In such cases, it might be worth removing the treatment in a reversal or ABAB design.

Fig. 7.3 is a sample reversal design graph evaluating a feeding intervention. There are several variations to reversal designs but all of them involve removing or discontinuing part or all of the treatment package after the treatment package has been shown to work. In a classic reversal design, you would go back to baseline and continue to implement baseline meals until the client's food consumption returns to baseline levels and remains stable there. This approach would require implementing a minimum of three baseline meals during the reversal phase but sometimes more. Another option that may be more clinically

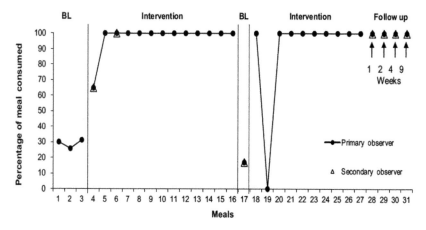

*Figure 7.4 Example of an ABAB design with a brief reversal. Note only a single reversal meal was necessary to clearly demonstrate the necessity of the treatment.* Reprinted with permission from West Virginia University Press.

appropriate is to implement a "brief reversal," which refers to a very short reversal to baseline phase that is just long enough to begin to show a disruption in feeding. Brief reversals can be as brief as a single meal, if an immediate decrease in feeding is observed. Fig. 7.4 depicts an example from our practice, in which we treated a child with ASD via a purely parent-mediated approach. We asked the client's mother to implement only a single baseline meal during the reversal phase. The client's consumption decreased to approximately 15%, and we immediately instructed his mother to return to treatment meals, at which point the client's consumption rapidly returned to 100% (Tarbox, Schiff, & Najdowski, 2011).

### 7.4.2.3 Alternating Treatments Design

Occasionally, when designing the potential intervention with the treatment team and parents, you may have trouble deciding which of two possible interventions is most likely to be most effective. A good option is to use an alternating treatments design (aka, multielement or multiple treatments design) to evaluate both and compare which is better. Fig. 7.5 is a sample alternating treatments design graph, comparing two feeding treatments. To implement an alternating treatments design, begin as usual with a brief baseline, simply to ensure that the client actually needs intervention to eat those foods. You then alternate meals back and forth between the two different treatments that you want to evaluate. You can

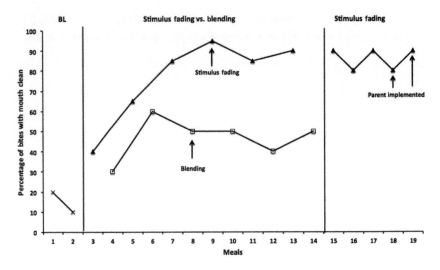

*Figure 7.5 Sample alternating treatments design comparison of two feeding treatments. Blending was compared to stimulus fading and stimulus fading was found to be more effective. The final phase implemented stimulus fading only and finished by training parents to implement treatment.*

alternate treatments back and forth (e.g., **ABABABA**) or you can semirandomize the sequence, with the rule that the same treatment is not conducted more than twice, consecutively (e.g., **ABBABAAB**). The former has the disadvantage of possible sequence effects and the latter has the disadvantage of requiring more planning effort. Continue alternating meals of both treatments until one or both treatments increase consumption to target levels (generally 80% or higher).

If both treatments work equally well, then choose the treatment that the parents and client prefer. If only one works and the other does not, drop the one that does not work and continue with the effective treatment. If neither works, you will need to either identify how one or both can be modified to be more effective or a third treatment should be implemented.

# CHAPTER 8

# Caregiver Training and Follow-Up

The purpose of all treatment in applied behavior analysis is to produce large socially meaningful behavior changes that endure across settings and time. In order for behavior change to generalize to all meaningful aspects of a client's life, it is critical to ensure that the client does not continue to depend on you for the improved behavior to continue to occur. This chapter describes practical procedures for transferring feeding treatment to caregivers and for ensuring that feeding gains generalize to all relevant aspects of the client's life. For children that live at home, caregivers could include their birth parents, grandparents, aunts, uncles, same-sex parents, adopted parents, foster parents, and so on. For clients who live in professionally managed residential settings, this could include direct care staff and others. For school-based consultation, the ongoing caregivers you will need to transfer treatment to will likely be teachers and paraprofessionals. We fully acknowledge that each client may have a unique living circumstance and, for the sake of clarity and brevity, we use the term "parents" in this chapter to refer to whoever the normal, ongoing caregivers are for the client with whom you are working.

## 8.1 CAREGIVER TRAINING

Training parents and other caregivers to take over feeding intervention is among the most critical parts of the feeding treatment process. Contrary to how it is sometimes approached, parent training is *not an afterthought.* As professional applied behavior analysis (ABA) therapists are not going to be responsible for feeding the client forever, training caregivers effectively is the primary factor that will determine whether you really solve the feeding problem on a long-term basis. Parent training has the broader and perhaps more important role of introducing caregivers to the power and generality of behavioral principles as well. It can be an incredibly powerful learning experience the first time that a parent witnesses the clear cause-and-effect relation that

Treating Feeding Challenges in Autism. DOI: http://dx.doi.org/10.1016/B978-0-12-813563-1.00008-2

occurs when they consistently follow-through with a behavioral intervention and their child's behavior changes accordingly. Repeatedly implementing and witnessing reinforcement contingencies help parents form their own general rules, along the lines of "What I do makes my child's behavior change," or "How I respond to my child's behavior determines how he will behave in the future," or "I have the power to help my child learn to behave better." The most research-proven method for training parents and other caregivers is behavioral skills training (BST), and this process was described in Chapter 7, Treatment Management, so it will not be repeated here. However, we discuss some of the more important variables that might impact your parent training and some of the approaches for implementing it below.

## 8.1.1 When to Include Parents

The first decision to make regarding transferring treatment to parents is when to begin. As described in the staffing section of Chapter 7, Treatment Management, parents can be included as early as the first day of treatment. However, the vast majority of professionals will choose to conduct most of the initial treatment themselves and then transfer the treatment to parents some time later. For this approach, there are perhaps two major choices.

### 8.1.1.1 Including Parents at the End

The first option for when to include parents in treatment is to wait until the client has met all major feeding goals with you and then train parents to implement the latest permutation of the intervention. If you choose this option, parents might wait for weeks or months to begin to do anything different from what they normally did during mealtimes with their child. It might be wise to have parents observe treatment meals with your staff during this time, so that they begin to learn about behavioral feeding procedures, well before they are trained to do them. An advantage of waiting this long to train parents to implement intervention is that the problem may be largely solved before parents dive in, so it may be less effortful for parents. In addition, many parents of children with feeding disorders experience severe distress surrounding feeding and may feel emotionally unprepared for the rigors of the early stages of behavioral intervention. Waiting to include parents until the end thereby gives some parents a much needed escape from stress surrounding feeding. A disadvantage to this option is that it effectively excludes parents from the active treatment process and therefore an opportunity for a powerful parent learning experience is lost. Another disadvantage is that some parents may feel impatient and dissatisfied by having to wait before becoming actively involved.

### 8.1.1.2 Step-Wise Inclusion of Parents

A great option for when to include parents is to train and include parents after each large milestone has been met with therapists. For example, consider a 4-year-old girl who ate no fruits or vegetables at intake. The first phase of treatment consisted of reinforcing eating each bite of vegetables with a bite of highly preferred animal crackers (i.e., FR1 reinforcement). During this first phase of treatment, parents were instructed to do nothing different than they normally did during mealtimes when therapists were absent. After the child consistently ate five new vegetables and five new fruits in this first treatment phase, parents were trained on how to implement the treatment and were asked to do so during one meal per day when therapists were absent. The supervisor met with the parents regularly to review the data they collected and supervise their implementation (after initial training, as described in Chapter 7: Treatment Management). Although the parents successfully implemented this first phase of treatment, the professional therapists began the second phase of treatment, which was thinning out positive reinforcement. During this phase, the bite requirement for earning animal crackers was gradually increased over successive meals, until the client ate an entire nutritious, well-balanced meal and then received a reasonable dessert. At this point, parents were trained on how to gradually thin out reinforcement during the meals they conducted in the absence of therapists and the supervisor continued to meet regularly with them to review data and supervise how the reinforcement thinning process worked with parents.

There is no fixed rule regarding the particular points at which you include parents in a step-wise fashion and the number of individual steps you choose to implement with parents. Like all other aspects of behavioral intervention, parent training and inclusion must be carefully planned, supervised, and problem solved. All other things being equal, asking parents to make smaller changes is more likely to be successful but will take longer.

## 8.1.2 Variables that Affect Parent Training

The prior amount of training and experience, if any, that a parent has with other behavioral intervention procedures will affect how easily parents acquire new feeding skills. For example, if parents can already clearly articulate how positive reinforcement and escape might be at work in feeding disorders, you may be able to spend less time on the first step of BST and might be able to move more quickly to modeling and role-playing specific procedures.

The number and type of other demands bearing on parents, in addition to feeding, will also likely have an effect. For example, if the client has multiple siblings that the parent is responsible for overseeing at the same time as implementing feeding intervention, that will present a major challenge. Similarly, if only one parent is responsible for most or all childcare and the other parent is partially or completely absent (functionally, even if not physically), that will also compound the challenges faced by the parent you are training. Expectations of parent training may therefore need to be adjusted. Training can be conducted in smaller steps and/or childcare may need to be arranged during training sessions.

### 8.1.2.1 Emotional Support for Parents

If parents are experiencing significant strife between one another, an unfortunately common circumstance in families of children with ASD, you might be wise to gently and compassionately refer them to a family therapist or licensed psychologist as a supplement to the training you are giving them. Behavior analysts and other clinicians who have not been appropriately trained to deliver marriage counseling and family therapy should not attempt to do so and should recognize the limits of their scope of practice. However, there are some things behavior analysts can do that are well within our scope of practice. First, being an empathetic listener is a critical part of interacting with any clients. When parents share their difficult emotions with you, consider making eye contact, listening carefully, and giving plenty of room in the conversation for the parent to share what they have to say. Acknowledge and validate the challenges they are facing, without pretending that you actually know from experience what it is like.

If you are not trained in counseling, you might notice yourself feeling uncomfortable when parents share their most difficult emotions with you. Consider noticing your own feelings of discomfort and making room for them. Just as it is natural for the parents of children with ASD to feel stress, it is natural for clinicians to feel distress when parents seem to be reaching out for something the clinician has not been trained to provide. It is worth recognizing for yourself that being an effective behavior analyst does not require that you *feel* confident in emotionally charged situations; it requires that you act with empathy and train parents in procedures that work and it is entirely possible for you to do this even when you feel uncomfortable. Put another way, giving parents the space to share their difficult emotions with you, without you trying to fix them, will not put you or your work as a behavior analyst at risk. To the contrary, it will likely help build trust with the parent so they are more likely to engage in the challenge of doing what you are trying to train them to do, even with their feelings of fear or hopelessness.

Although it is not within the scope of practice of behavioral feeding intervention to deliver couples counseling, some basic behavioral recommendations can help foster support among couples, rather than strife. For example, it can be helpful to recommend to each parent to notice at least one thing that their significant other does well each day and acknowledge it in some genuine way, whether that be a thank you, a hug, or making them a cup of coffee, etc. Another helpful recommendation is for each parent to designate some very small part of their week or day that is purely for themselves. For example, after the children go to sleep, their mom might attend a yoga class or go for a walk or watch their favorite television program.

### 8.1.3 Incorporating Values

Whenever and however you begin the parent training process, consider incorporating parent's values from the start. Implementing behavioral feeding procedures can be very difficult for parents to do and connecting them to values can be helpful. By values, we mean larger, overarching goals that transcend the details of daily life. Values are what we want to be about in life. Our deepest values are things that we are not willing to give up on, no matter how hard we are challenged. For many behavior analysts, examples of values that guide our daily professional lives are contributing to science, helping others achieve better lives, and making the world a better place. Many exercises have been developed in the acceptance and commitment therapy literature (Luoma, Hayes, & Walser, 2007), that help us and our clients identify and work with values.

One exercise to help parents identify their values related to their child's feeding disorder is to ask them to imagine they are at a dinner celebrating their child's college graduation (or some other important event that celebrates the client, like 40th birthday party, etc.). Now ask the parent to imagine they have to give a speech that describes all of their child's proudest characteristics and accomplishments. Ask the parent to take a few minutes and write down the top three or five. Parents might write down things like they want their child to be hard-working, a good friend, a good spouse, etc. You can then validate what the parent writes down by saying something like, "Okay, excellent, so it sounds like you have identified some of the values that matter the most to you in raising your child. It seems like maybe you are telling me that these are the things that matter the most to you as a parent? These are some of the things that you are willing to fight for." Then choose one of the values and identify how doing the feeding treatment is going to help their child move in the direction of that value. For example, "So it sounds like your child having strong rela-tionships matters a lot to you. Let's talk about how her feeding connects with those values. If we don't fix this feeding issue and your child still only eats five foods when she is 5 or 10 or 20 years old, do you think it's going to affect her ability to make and keep friends? Definitely. When she gets invited to that first sleepover with friends but she has a tantrum because they serve the wrong food, that's not going to help her make friends, right?" After the parent makes the con-nection between the feeding treatment now and their child's movement toward what the parent values for them in the future, you can con-clude the exercise with some kind of summary statement, e.g., "Okay, so it sounds like putting in the hard work now can move your child toward a greater future later, let's do it!"

### 8.1.4 Short-Term Versus Long-Term Outcomes

In addition to connecting parent training with values as described above, it can be very useful to talk to parents about short-term versus long-term outcomes of how we deal with feeding problems. The classic behavioral functional analysis of caregiver−client interactions around escape-maintained challenging behavior, whether feeding-related or not, is that both the parent and the child are "working for" short-term negative reinforcement, usually without even knowing it. Specifically, when the parent asks the child to eat something they do not want to eat, the child misbehaves because misbehavior produces immediate negative reinforcement in the form of escape from eating the nonpre-ferred food. And of course, when the child misbehaves, that is aversive to the parent, and if the parent allows the child to escape eating, then the child's misbehavior stops and thus the parent escapes their child misbehaving, which then negatively reinforces the parent's behavior of allowing their child to escape eating.

The scenario above was discussed in more detail in Chapter 2, Medical and Behavioral Origins of Feeding Problems, on the behavioral origins of feeding disorders. It is a critically important part of the first step of BST with parents to describe and discuss this negative reinforcement relationship for both parent and client. However, it is also helpful to then relate it to the values you identified with the parent, if you choose to work on clarifying values. By definition, values are long-term, so it can be helpful to talk to parents about immediate negative reinforcement versus long-term positive reinforcement. For example, it might be useful to say something like:

> Doing this feeding intervention could be one of the toughest things you will ever have to do as a parent, barring any major medical disasters. You can choose to avoid that struggle by continuing to let your child eat whatever they want. And no one would blame you for it. You are facing enough as it is. But I wonder whether it would be worth it to lean into the challenge, to struggle even more, if it got you closer to that outcome that you care so much about later on? I wonder if it would be worth it to forgo the small reward of avoiding tantrums today if it would have the eventual much larger reward of seeing your child eating a healthy variety of foods and all of the benefits that will give him later? I wonder if one of the greatest gifts you can give your child is to not give him what he wants right now, to follow through and not let him escape eating new foods?

Be careful with your words when you are talking to parents about these bigger values and their behavior in relation to them. Do not come off as judgmental or critical. Do not act like it should be easy for parents to make these tough choices. You need to approach this kind of discussion with empathy and care and it's important to not make it seem like you "have it all figured out." Make it clear you know you are just a clinician doing your best to help a parent do their best.

## 8.2 COLLABORATION WITH OTHER PROFESSIONALS

In Chapters 2 and 3, we discussed the importance of assessments conducted by medical and other professionals to ensure the client is safe to work on feeding and that her feeding disorder is not otherwise explained by a medical problem. Collaborating with other disciplines is equally important during the follow-up phase of treatment. As clients have success with feeding intervention and their repertoire of foods increases in number and variety, parents will need to make decisions about when to fade out supplemental feedings, if any, and when an adequate variety of foods from each food group have been accomplished. Parents should be encouraged to seek consultation from a nutritionist during this time, if they have not done so already. In more medically involved cases, such as clients who still depend on a g-tube for some of their calories, parents will need to make decisions about when to fade the frequency and amount of tube feedings. Decisions about tube feedings should not be made by behavior analysts; parents should seek guidance from medical professionals.

Behavior analysts should also consider seeking consultation from speech pathologists and/or occupational therapists throughout the treatment process and during the follow-up phase. In particular, if the success of your feeding treatment stalls, consultation from other disciplines may be especially wise. In addition, collaborating with other professionals in your client's school or vocational setting will be an important part of the follow-up and fade-out process. We discussed models for school-based consultation treatment of feeding disorders in Chapter 7, Treatment Management but collaboration with and training of school staff is equally important if the school staff are to carry out follow-up and maintenance of treatment gains.

## 8.3 PLANNING FOR GENERALIZATION AND MAINTENANCE

### 8.3.1 Generalization

In Chapter 3, Preparing for Meals, we discussed how to program for generalization from the very start of your feeding intervention. If you have done this vigorously, then generalization during the follow-up phase of treatment may be less challenging. If you have not, generalization may present a more significant challenge. Regardless, during the process of fading-out professionally delivered feeding intervention, you will need to carefully plan for, execute, and monitor the extent to which the gains of feeding intervention generalize to all other relevant aspects of the client's daily life. Keep in mind that, by definition, generalization means the spreading of the effects of intervention across some untrained variable. Therefore, if you directly train a parent to implement intervention and they do so effectively in the context in which you trained them to do it, that is not really generalization for the parent or the client; that is the client and parent doing what they were directly trained to do. What we really strive for with generalization is the client and the parent demonstrating their skills in settings in which they were not directly trained. For example, after sufficient training with you, the parent should be able to implement meals without you present, in which they introduce a new food, or conduct a meal in a new room of the house or at a new restaurant, or present the meal with new plates or in a different chair, and so on, with the client still eating successfully, despite these changes.

As discussed in Chapter 3, Preparing for Meals, the most reliable procedure for producing generalization is multiple exemplar training across foods, rooms of the house, adults implementing the meal, and so on. The same is true during the parent's training and follow-up phases. It is all-too-easy for parents and clinicians (and clients!) to become comfortable with routines but routines are bad for generalization. Even in the beginning of parent training, as soon as the client is successful, consider changing foods/settings/etc., on the next meal that the parent conducts.

### 8.3.2 Maintenance

Maintenance is the persistence of improvements in feeding and reductions in mealtime challenging behaviors after the formal treatment phase is over. Maintenance is often treated as an afterthought and it may not be as interesting as treatment but, like generalization, it is just as important. Treatment is all but useless if the treatment gains do not maintain. Three strategies for ensuring maintenance will be described below: (1) training others, (2) programming for maintenance, and (3) fading treatment.

### 8.3.2.1 Training Others

The importance of training other caregivers, including parents, school staff, residential staff and others, has already been discussed at length. However, it is important when fading out your formal feeding treatment and transitioning the responsibility for it to others, to make a formal maintenance plan. The maintenance plan should specify who is going to be responsible for conducting meals after your team is done, what procedures are to be used during those meals, and specifications as to how to troubleshoot if problems arise in the future. Furthermore, it should specify how often follow-up visits are to be conducted by the supervising behavior analyst and how parents should email data to document ongoing success.

### 8.3.2.2 Programing for Maintenance

Many of the same procedures that are useful for programing for generalization are also useful for programing for maintenance because maintenance can actually be thought about as a special kind of generalization: generalization across time. We will not repeat our recommendations regarding generalization here, but we encourage you to look over the generalization procedures described in that section when programing for maintenance. Two other variables are also worth considering: (1) reinforcement history and (2) intermittent reinforcement.

Research from the behavioral momentum literature suggests that behaviors that have earned more reinforcement in the past are more resistant to change than behaviors that have earned less reinforcement (Nevin & Shahan, 2011). Although most of this research has been basic laboratory research, it has important applied implications. What it suggests is that it may be very important to make sure that the desirable behavior change that you have produced has received a lengthy and rich history of reinforcement before fading treatment out and hoping that it maintains. So, all other things being equal, more successful treatment meals containing rich reinforcement for varied and flexible eating are better than fewer, before considering when to fade out your intervention.

Intermittent reinforcement is a commonly used strategy to promote maintenance of behavior change. Earlier phases of treatment meals often reinforce every occurrence of eating nonpreferred foods, that is, they implement positive reinforcement on an FR1 schedule. This is an effective approach to intervention and it helps build the rich reinforcement history for eating that the behavioral momentum literature suggests is necessary. However, before expecting improved eating to maintain, you should consider thinning the reinforcement schedule. After FR1 positive reinforcement has been implemented for a substantial amount of time, you could transition to an FR2 schedule, where the client needs to eat two consecutive bites of nonpreferred food before earning a positive reinforcer. You could then thin the schedule of reinforcement to FR3, FR4, FR5, and so on, until you reach a leaner schedule. You may also choose to switch to a

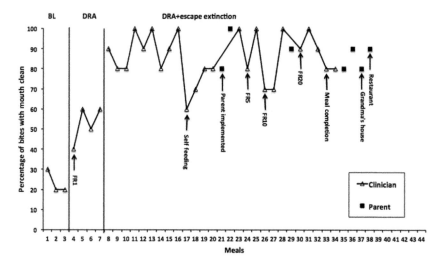

*Figure 8.1 Sample graph showing the full life of a treatment, including baseline, initial evaluation of DRA, adding escape extinction, thinning out the positive reinforcement schedule, training parents to implement meals, and generalizing to additional home and community settings.*

variable ratio (VR) schedule, where the exact number of bites required for reinforcement is unpredictable but averages around some specific number. For example, you might implement something along the lines of the following schedule: FR1, FR2, VR2, VR3, VR5, VR7, VR10, VR15, and then VR20. Such reinforcement schedules probably resemble reinforcement contingencies in the real world and they may be especially effective for encouraging maintenance. You can also use the same schedule-thinning strategy to gradually increase the number of nonpreferred bites required to be eaten until the meal is terminated (Fig. 8.1).

Regardless of how you choose to thin your reinforcement schedule, remember that you should only thin it further when the client's feeding is successful and stable at the current parameter. There are no strict rules for how to progress through schedule thinning. The faster you thin, the more likely the client is to be unsuccessful, and the slower you thin, the longer the process will take. The process should be governed by visual inspection of the data after every meal.

### 8.3.2.3 Fading Treatment Out

With many feeding interventions, you may not necessarily bring the client's feeding habits completely on par with his typically developing peers and the parents and treatment team may be just fine with that. For example, a mother may decide that, as long as there are at least five different foods from each food group that her child will eat, that is enough for her to manage her family meals reasonably successfully. Your professionally delivered treatment phase may then end when that goal has been reached and you may then start the caregiver training and follow-up phase, wherein the next goal is to fade your team out. You might then train all relevant caregivers in the treatment procedures that your team ended with, working on the assumption that the client's everyday caregivers will continue to use those procedures indefinitely, or until they request another intervention by your team to move the client's feeding to the next level. In short, there are cases in which there is no need to fade treatment out—maintenance simply consists of the parents continuing to implement treatment after the professional team is done.

In other cases, the parents and your team may decide that it may be possible for the client to achieve successful feeding without specialized support. In order to achieve this goal, your team will need to fade the treatment out. Treatment fading is a technique for enhancing maintenance, but it is not quite the same thing as maintaining an intervention; it is the systematic *removal* of the intervention. Treatment fading has scarcely been researched and so there is very little research to draw recommendations from. However, in our clinical experience, many of the children we have worked with have had their feeding interventions completely faded out, gradually over time.

| Feeder | Clinician-Fed      Parent-Fed      Self-Fed |
|---|---|
| Reinforcement Schedule | FR1 FR2 FR4 FR8 FR10 FR15 FR20 FR30 |
| Reinforcer Amount | One Bite      One Reasonable Dessert |
| Bites per Meal | 10 15 20 25  30 Age Appropriate Meal Size |
| Texture | Baby Food   Ground   Chopped Fine Age Appropriate |
| Total New Foods | 4 8 12 16 20 30 50 Age Appropriate Variety |
| Setting | Highchair  Chair at Table   Fully Included in Family Meals |
| Weeks of Intervention | 1 5  10 15  20 25  30 35  40 45  50 |

Many of the procedures discussed in the maintenance and schedule-thinning sections of the book are relevant to treatment fading and they work on the same basic logic: gradually altering the client's environment from that which constituted the full treatment package to something more closely resembling normal everyday life. The most important general principle to keep in mind is gradual fading. All aspects of an intervention package can be gradually faded. The frequency of professionally delivered meals can be faded out. The duration, bite requirement, or novelty of meals can be faded up. Even parent's involvement in meals can be gradually faded out. For example, if the client's father begins implementing the feeding treatment sitting with the client for the entire meal and delivering positive reinforcement after each bite, treatment may be faded by thinning out the positive reinforcement schedule and then by fading the father's presence out. The father could be faded out of the meal starting with the last bite of the meal, where the client is required to feed himself the bite. Then the last two, then the last three, etc., until the father "checks in" on the client intermittently, like he might normally do with the client's typically developing siblings.

### 8.3.2.4 Self-Feeding
An important component to treatment fading will be to transition from a nonself-feeding to a self-feeding format (Piazza, Anderson, & Fisher, 1993). Start with foods your client readily accepts. Occasionally, just providing a food established during the nonself-feeding format will result in your client feeding herself a bite. Or you may need to prestab or prescoop the bite and then provide an instruction to "take a bite." In some cases, self-feeding will need to be completely taught using prompting and reinforcement. Although there is very little published research on teaching self-feeding, well established prompting and reinforcement procedures can be applied. We have had success using a 3-step guided compliance/prompting procedure. To use 3-step to teach self-feeding, present the bite on the utensil with a vocal prompt (e.g., "Take a bite"). If the client does not feed himself the bite after approximately 5 seconds, move to the vocal plus model prompt (e.g., "Take a bite like this," while modeling accepting a bite of food from the utensil). If the client still does not feed himself the bite, provide a vocal prompt plus physical guidance (e.g., "This is how you take your bite,") while manually guiding the client's hand to grasp the utensil and bring it to his mouth. Be careful to use the minimum force necessary. You are not force-feeding the client; you are merely using physical guidances to help the client execute the self-feeding behavior.

### 8.3.2.5 Regular Family Meals

We recommend trying to incorporate the client's family's regular daily routines into the goals of the feeding intervention. Initial feeding treatment meals are often conducted with only the client and one adult (clinician at first, transitioning to the parent), at a different time and sometimes a different room from the normal family meal. For the early stages of treatment, this may be reasonable, as the primary concern is to create the least distracting, most easily controlled environment to treat feeding difficulties. However, this also inherently segregates the client from the rest of her family and so it should be faded, whenever possible. You might begin by fading the other aspects of the client's treatment first, for example, thinning the reinforcement schedule, fading to normal bite sizes, fading to self-feeding, and so on. Once the client's meal looks as close to a regular family meal as it is going to be, you (or a parent) might try it at the table with the rest of the family present.

# CHAPTER 9

# Troubleshooting

Behavioral interventions for feeding disorders tend to be very effective. In fact, we have yet to meet an individual whose behavioral feeding problem was not amenable to improvement via behavioral intervention, although we may of course meet such a person someday. Despite the very reliable effectiveness of behavioral approaches, nothing is perfect and do not expect treatment to always progress with zero setbacks. Especially if you treat the more severe cases and especially if you do it for very long, expect everything that you think works to not work at some point. In this chapter, we provide practical advice for how to troubleshoot some of the more common setbacks you are likely to encounter. Keep in mind that this book is not intended to address highly medically involved feeding cases, so we do not address problems that are primarily medical in nature. As we discussed in Chapter 2, Medical and Behavioral Origins of Feeding Problems, make sure the client undergoes a thorough medical evaluation before you begin feeding treatment so that you do not run into feeding failures that are primarily medical in nature and/or expose your client to undue risk by treating someone who is not safe to receive feeding treatment.

## 9.1 PROBLEMATIC BEHAVIORS

It is rare to treat a feeding disorder that does not include problematic behaviors of some sort. Just as it is common for individuals with autism to display some level of food selectivity, it is also very common for that food selectivity to be accompanied by problematic behaviors during meals, especially in the beginning stages of treatment.

### 9.1.1 Expels

As described in Chapter 3, Preparing for Meals, expels include pushing food or liquid out of the mouth (i.e., past the plane of the lips) after it has been accepted into the mouth (i.e., "spitting" the food out). The consequence you will implement for expels will vary depending on the

Treating Feeding Challenges in Autism. DOI: http://dx.doi.org/10.1016/B978-0-12-813563-1.00009-4

behavioral feeding treatment you are conducting. For example, differential reinforcement of alternative behavior (DRA) for acceptance involves reinforcement for acceptance of bites and does not include any planned consequences for expelled bites. So, an expelled bite would simply be ignored, although when implementing escape extinction, an expelled bite is most often represented to prevent escape from swallowing the bite.

If your client is engaging in a high rate of expelled bites and this rate is stable or increasing consistently, it is likely time to reexamine your intervention. Occasionally, an antecedent variable may be effective in reducing expels. For example, including stimulus fading or texture fading as a component of your treatment package sometimes decreases expels. For one client we worked with, all that was needed to eliminate expelling of vegetables was to add a nutritionally acceptable amount of salt. You may also want to implement a specific differential reinforcement contingency, such as providing reinforcement for not expelling (i.e., differential reinforcement of other behavior (DRO)), to teach your client not to engage in expelling bites. Don't be afraid to include additional treatment components when troubleshooting, as they can usually be faded over the course of intervention.

If you have tried other options and they have not worked, it may be necessary to implement escape extinction specifically for expels, consisting of representation of expelled bites, if you are not already doing so. To do this, simply scoop-up expelled bites and immediately represent them. If the expelled food falls on the floor or is otherwise not available for representation, present a new bite of the same food immediately. Fig. 9.1 depicts hypothetical data from a feeding intervention that is working to increase acceptance but the client is expelling most of the accepted bites. Adding representation of expelled bites decreases expelling and therefore increases consumption.

### 9.1.2 Packing

Packing is another problematic behavior that may affect your client's progress. A pack includes any food remaining (i.e., more than about the size of a pea) in the client's mouth more than 30 seconds after acceptance. Packing often results in delayed or less swallowing of foods, which may affect an individual's caloric or nutrient intake and/or make meals last long enough to become a problem for the family. Packing also increases the risk for choking or aspiration, thus, reducing this behavior will likely be important when the behavior occurs. As with expels, antecedent

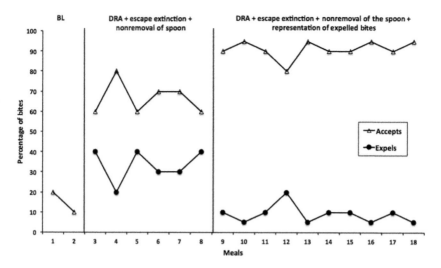

*Figure 9.1 Sample graph of a feeding intervention that increases food acceptance but that is failing because the client is expelling food. Adding the procedural component of representing expelled bites decreases expelling and therefore increases consumption.*

variables such as stimulus fading or texture fading may be effective in reducing packing.

Redistribution is another option to decrease packing. Redistribution is when the clinician moves food that the client has packed in his mouth. Often, clients will pack food by holding it in the sides of their mouths. Redistribution is then used to move the food from the cheeks back to the tongue, providing the opportunity to chew and swallow the food. Most commonly, a bristled Nuk® brush is used to collect the remaining food from the client's cheek by placing the brush under the food and scooping, then placing the food in the middle of the client's tongue, rotating the brush while removing it from the client's mouth to deposit the food on his tongue. Redistribution has been shown to effectively reduce packing (Gulotta, Piazza, Patel, & Layer, 2005). It should be noted that clients will often prefer to not have their bites redistributed and it can therefore be quite an intrusive treatment option. We recommend only doing this procedure after you have been directly trained by someone else who is an expert. In addition, we recommend first trying other options for decreasing packing.

### 9.1.3 Vomiting
The vast majority of feeding clients do not vomit but it does occasionally occur, so you should be prepared to carefully track it when it

happens. The first time that a particular client vomits during feeding intervention, we recommend terminating the meal but be very careful to not react any more than is needed to maintain safety and dignity. There is no need to draw undue attention to the behavior, as it is important to avoid shaping up an attention function. Of course, by terminating the meal, you are giving the client an escape from eating the remainder of the nonpreferred food, so you run the risk of turning vomiting into an escape maintained behavior. If vomiting continues to occur, we recommend that you refer your client to a medical doctor to assess possible medical problems. If medical causes of vomiting have been conclusively ruled out and it appears that vomiting is motivated by escape from eating, you can consider not terminating meals when vomiting occurs. Keep in mind that this decision will appear unreasonable to most people and you need to be completely sure that this option is safe for your client and of course obtain parental permission before doing it.

### 9.1.4 Gagging

Gagging often occurs early on in feeding intervention. It is most common to observe gagging when new foods are introduced and/or when a client first experiences a novel taste or texture. Repeated exposure to foods usually results in a reduction in gagging. You can often decrease gagging faster by implementing antecedent components, such as stimulus fading or texture fading. In the majority of cases, however, it is not necessary to do anything specific for gagging. If you simply ignore it, if often goes away, but we recommend collecting data on it so that you can objectively track whether it is getting better or worse over time. Interestingly, foods that at first elicit gagging often cease to do so later, and can even become preferred foods even later on in treatment.

### 9.1.5 Discontinuing Target Foods

Although we recommend selecting target foods and remaining consistent, we also recommend taking individual preference into account. That is, not every person is going to enjoy eating every food; we all have some foods we really enjoy eating and other foods we choose not to eat. If you introduce a certain food and note that the client finds it much more highly nonpreferred than other target foods, you can consider not including that food in future treatment meals. As long as the client learns to eat a large enough variety of foods, it is probably not worth the battle to push that particular food. However, we do not recommend discontinuing a food in the middle of a meal, because you could easily accidentally reinforce refusal behavior by removing that food from the meal. Obviously, any new foods that the team learns the client is allergic to should be excluded. In addition, we recommend being flexible about reasonable events in the client's life (e.g., you may want to change food in order to target specific foods in preparation for a trip to the grandparents' house). Overall, we recommend running treatment sessions according to protocol, then reviewing data and making any food changes based on the data and on a reasonable assessment of the big picture.

## 9.1.6 Discontinuation of Intervention

Just like any intervention, feeding treatment must be discontinued immediately if it is not safe for the client. Unsafe situations might include challenging behavior that you are not able to safely manage (e.g., intense self-injurious behavior that is harming the client) or if the client is experiencing medical problems (e.g., allergic reactions, digestion problems, etc.). In some circumstances, parents may choose to terminate feeding treatment for individual reasons (e.g., stress involved, time necessary, etc.).

In some cases, the progress made might be enough to stop treatment in order to prioritize treatment time to other behaviors. This may sometimes be the case if treatment is being done as part of a larger comprehensive applied behavior analysis (ABA) program. For example, if 10 hours of a 40 hour per week ABA program are being used to target feeding, once the client has achieved meaningful gains in feeding behaviors, those 10 hours might be better used to target other relevant behaviors, even if terminal feeding objectives have not yet been fully achieved. Additional funding limitations, such as reduced funding or unexpected loss of funding, might also affect access to feeding treatment.

As with any treatment, feeding intervention should be discontinued if the client does not make, or no longer makes, measurable and meaningful treatment gains. However, in our personal experience, we have never witnessed a feeding intervention that needed to be terminated because it was not possible to make meaningful progress. If your client is not progressing sufficiently, we recommend seeking consultation and mentorship from another clinician who has substantially more experience in treating feeding disorders.

# CONCLUSION

We hope you have found this book useful in your endeavors at helping individuals with autism spectrum disorder (ASD) learn to love eating a healthier variety of foods. Eating is one of the great pleasures of life, and we believe that individuals with ASD have a right to access that source of pleasure, just like everyone else does. Keep in mind that the big picture take home points are to rely heavily on positive reinforcement, use lots of antecedent modifications, fade treatment components in and out slowly, and focus heavily on caregiver training, generalization, and maintenance. Although the particular procedures used in feeding treatment are somewhat unique, they are all based on and work because of, basic behavioral principles of learning and motivation. If you keep this in mind, you will rarely go astray. Feeding treatment can be difficult and, ironically, unappetizing at times, but it can also be a great source of satisfaction because the effects you can have are among the most dramatic you can obtain in helping professions. We wish you the best of luck in treating feeding disorders. May you have a future filled with many happy meals for you, your clients, and your family.

# Further Reading

## BOOK CHAPTERS

Fodstad, J. C., McCourt, S., Minor, L. R., & Minshawi, N. F. (2016). Feeding disorders. In J. Matson (Ed.), *Comorbid conditions among children with autism spectrum disorders* (pp. 187–216). New York: Springer International Publishing.

Milnes, S. M., & Piazza, C. C. (2013). Intensive treatment of pediatric feeding disorders. In D. D. Reed, F. D. DiGennaro Reed, & J. Luiselli (Eds.), *Handbook of crisis intervention and developmental disabilities* (pp. 393–408). New York: Springer.

Piazza, C. C., Roane, H. S., & Kadey, H. J. (2009). Treatment of pediatric feeding disorders. In J. M. Matson, F. Andrasik, & M. L. Matson (Eds.), *Treating childhood psychopathology and developmental disabilities* (pp. 435–444). New York: Springer.

Vaz, P. C., & Piazza, C. C. (2010). Behavioural approaches to the management of paediatric feeding disorders. In A. Southall, & C. Martin (Eds.), *Feeding problems in children. A practical guide* (pp. 53–73). London: Radcliffe Publishing.

## BOOKS

Williams, K. E., & Foxx, R. M. (2007). *Treating eating problems of children with autism spectrum disorders and developmental disabilities*. Austin, TX: Pro-Ed.

## JOURNAL ARTICLES

Matson, J. L., & Fodstad, J. C. (2009). The treatment of food selectivity and other feeding problems in children with autism spectrum disorders. *Research in Autism Spectrum Disorders, 3*(2), 455–461.

Sharp, W. G., Jaquess, D. L., Morton, J. F., & Herzinger, C. V. (2010). Pediatric feeding disorders: A quantitative synthesis of treatment outcomes. *Clinical Child and Family Psychology Review, 13*(4), 348–365.

Williams, K. E., Field, D. G., & Seiverling, L. (2010). Food refusal in children: A review of the literature. *Research in Developmental Disabilities, 31*(3), 625–633.

# Sample Feeding Protocol

## POSITIVE REINFORCEMENT + SIZE FADING + REINFORCER MAGNITUDE + NONREMOVAL OF SPOON

**Client**: Jack, 2 years old     **Date Created/Revised:** 01/01/2017

### Purpose
To teach the client to eat a wider variety of foods, for the purposes of increasing the nutritiousness of his diet and expanding the variety of foods that he enjoys eating.

### Before Mealtime
- Parents should weigh client at least one time per week
- Reserve highly preferred reinforcers (edible and/or nonedible) that the client will not have access to outside of feeding program
- Wash hands before meals
- Prepare plastic plates/bowls, utensils, target foods, and reinforcers before a meal begins. Place small amount of each in separate cups. Consult notes from previous therapist and from Board Certified Behavior Analyst (BCBA) for what foods to target before each meal
- Cut food into prespecified bite sizes (see protocol below)
- Ensure client is hungry/has not eaten for at least 2 hours prior to treatment meal
- Assess preference to identify highly preferred reinforcers client will be earning during that meal

## MEALTIME PROTOCOL

### Escape Baseline
- Have client sit in high chair (buckled in with tray on)
- Present terminal (age appropriate) sized bite of target food and say, "Take a bite"

- Rotate through all foods presenting one bite of each before repeating
- As soon as the client opens his mouth to accept a bite, place spoon/ bite in his mouth and immediately provide verbal praise
- If client bats, turns head, cries, etc., remove the bite. Ignore expels
- Present a bite approximately every 30 seconds
- If this phase did not produce adequate improvements in feeding, move to the next phase

## DRA for Acceptance
- Implement all same procedures as previous phase with the addition of:
  - State contingencies with each bite presentation (e.g., "first bite, then chocolate")
  - Provide a reinforcer contingent on acceptance of bite
- If this phase did not produce adequate improvements in feeding, move to the next phase

## DRA for Acceptance + Size Fading + Reinforcer Magnitude
- Implement all same procedures as previous treatment phase with the addition of:
  - Present VERY small bites of food, one at a time (start with one-eighth of a bite of food for each bite)
  - Increase reinforcer magnitude (e.g., duration of access to iPad or toy, number of M&Ms, etc.)
- If this phase did not produce adequate improvements in feeding, move to the next phase

## DRA for Acceptance + Size Fading + Reinforcer Magnitude + Nonremoval of the Spoon
- Implement all same procedures as previous treatment phase with the addition of:
  - Hold bite of food immediately in front of (but not touching) his lips until accepted into mouth
  - If a bite is spilled, immediately scoop another to replace
  - Ignore problem behaviors, including expels. Do not negotiate or otherwise give attention to maladaptive behaviors.

## Treatment Fading

- As client successfully eats target foods, the size of bites will gradually be increased to age appropriate size, based on visual inspection of data
- Over repeated successful meals, decrease magnitude of reinforcement and thin reinforcement schedule
- After substantial progress has been made, parents will be directly trained to implement the intervention
  - The BCBA will be present for initial parent training and parent implementation and will fade out until the parents are successfully implementing meals at home, without professional assistance.
- Intervention to be generalized across foods, people, and settings

## Data

- **Acceptance**
  - **5 seconds:** Record a plus if the client accepts the bite within 5 seconds from presentation
  **OR**
  - **>5 seconds:** Record a plus if the client accepts the bite more than 5 seconds from presentation
- **Result**
  - **Mouth clean:** Record a plus if the client swallows entire bite within 30 seconds from acceptance
  - **Pack:** Record a plus if the client holds food in mouth after 30 seconds from acceptance
- **Feeding behaviors:** Record a plus if the client engages in expel, gag, or vomit behaviors
- **Problem behaviors:** Record each instance of head turns and bats. Take descriptive notes about any other challenging behaviors that occur.

# Sample Feeding Protocol

## NONCONTINGENT REINFORCEMENT +
## NONEXCLUSIONARY TIMEOUT + NONREMOVAL OF SPOON

**Client**: Johnny, 6 years old      **Date Created/Revised**: 01/01/2017

## Purpose

To teach the client to eat a wider variety of foods, for the purposes of increasing the nutritiousness of his diet and expanding the variety of foods that he enjoys eating.

## Before Mealtime

- Parents should weigh client at least one time per week
- Reserve highly preferred reinforcers (edible and/or nonedible) that the client will not have access to outside of feeding program
- Wash hands before meals
- Prepare plastic plates/bowls, utensils, target foods, and reinforcers before a meal begins. Place small amount of each in separate cups. Consult notes from previous therapist and from Board Certified Behavior Analyst (BCBA) for what foods to target before each meal
- Cut food into prespecified bite sizes (see protocol below)
- Ensure client is hungry/has not eaten for at least 2 hours prior to treatment meal
- Assess preference to identify highly preferred reinforcers.

## MEALTIME PROTOCOL

### Escape Baseline

- Have client sit in chair at table
- Present terminal (age appropriate) sized bite of target food and say, "Take a bite"

- Rotate through all foods presenting one bite of each before repeating
- As soon as the client opens his mouth to accept a bite, place spoon/bite in his mouth and immediately provide verbal praise
- If client bats, turns head, cries, etc., remove the bite. Ignore expels
- Present a bite approximately every 30 seconds
- If this phase did not produce adequate improvements in feeding, move to the next phase.

### Noncontingent Reinforcement
- Implement all same procedures as previous phase with the addition of:
  - Provide continuous access to highly preferred reinforcer from beginning of meal.
- If this phase did not produce adequate improvements in feeding, move to the next phase.

### Noncontingent Reinforcement + Nonexclusionary Timeout
- Implement all same procedures as previous treatment phase with the addition of:
  - If client refuses a bite, remove the reinforcer
  - Present the next bite. Provide access to the reinforcer contingent on acceptance of the bite
  - Continuous access to the reinforcer continues as long as bites are accepted
  - If no bites are accepted after the reinforcer is removed, it remains removed from the meal.
- If this phase did not produce adequate improvements in feeding, move to the next phase.

### Noncontingent Reinforcement + Nonexclusionary Timeout + Nonremoval of the Spoon
- Implement all same procedures as previous treatment phase with the addition of:
  - Hold bite of food immediately in front of (but not touching) his lips until accepted into mouth
  - If a bite is spilled, immediately scoop another to replace
  - Ignore problem behaviors, including expels. Do not negotiate or otherwise give attention to maladaptive behaviors.

## Treatment Fading

- Over repeated successful meals, the reinforcement scheduled will be thinned
- After substantial progress has been made, parents will be directly trained to implement the intervention
  - The BCBA will be present for initial parent training and parent implementation and will fade out until the parents are successfully implementing meals at home, without professional assistance.
- Intervention to be generalized across foods, people, and settings.


## Data

- **Acceptance**
  - **5 seconds:** Record a plus if the client accepts the bite within 5 seconds from presentation
  **OR**
  - **>5 seconds:** Record a plus if the client accepts the bite more than 5 seconds from presentation
- **Result**
  - **Mouth clean:** Record a plus if the client swallows entire bite within 30 seconds from acceptance
  - **Pack:** Record a plus if the client holds food in mouth after 30 seconds from acceptance
- **Feeding behaviors:** Record a plus if the client engages in expel, gag, or vomit behaviors
- **Problem behaviors:** Record each instance of head turns and bats. Take descriptive notes about any other challenging behaviors that occur.

# Sample Feeding Protocol

## POSITIVE REINFORCEMENT + SIZE FADING + NONREMOVAL OF THE MEAL

**Client:** Cleo, 4 years old    **Date Created/Revised:** 01/01/2017

### Purpose

To teach the client to eat a wider variety of foods, for the purposes of increasing the nutritiousness of her diet and expanding the variety of foods that she enjoys eating.

### Before Mealtime

- Parents should weigh client at least one time per week
- Reserve highly preferred reinforcers (edible and/or nonedible) that the client will not have access to outside of feeding program
- Wash hands before meals
- Prepare plastic plates/bowls, utensils, target foods, and reinforcers before a meal begins. Place small amount of each in separate cups. Consult notes from previous therapist and from Board Certified Behavior Analyst (BCBA) for what foods to target before each meal
- Cut food into prespecified bite sizes (see protocol below)
- Ensure client is hungry/has not eaten for at least 2 hours prior to treatment meal
- Assess preference to identify highly preferred reinforcers.

## MEALTIME PROTOCOL

### Escape Baseline

- Have client sit in chair at table
- Present terminal (age appropriate) sized bite of target food and say, "Take a bite"

- Rotate through all foods presenting one bite of each before repeating
- As soon as the client opens her mouth to accept a bite, place spoon/bite in her mouth and immediately provide verbal praise
- If client bats, turns head, cries, etc., remove the bite. Ignore expels.
- Present a bite approximately every 30 seconds
- If this phase did not produce adequate improvements in feeding, move to the next phase.

## DRA for Mouth Clean
- Implement all same procedures as previous phase with the addition of:
  - State contingencies with each bite presentation (e.g., "first bite, then iPad")
  - Provide a reinforcer contingent on mouth clean
- If this phase did not produce adequate improvements in feeding, move to the next phase.

## DRA for Mouth Clean + Size Fading
- Implement all same procedures as previous treatment phase with the addition of:
  - Present VERY small bites of food, one at a time (start with one-eighth of a bite of food for each bite)
- If this phase did not produce adequate improvements in feeding, move to the next phase.

## DRA for Mouth Clean + Size Fading + Nonremoval of the Meal
- Implement all same procedures as previous treatment phase with the addition of:
  - Client remains at meal setting until she consumes the required amount of food
  - If a bite is spilled, immediately scoop another to replace
  - Ignore problem behaviors, including expels. Do not negotiate or otherwise give attention to maladaptive behaviors
  - If the client needs to use the bathroom while refusing food, take her to the bathroom and then return to the meal
  - If the client waits 60 minutes without eating the entire meal, give her a 5 minute break away from the table, with no preferred toys or attention, and then return to the table to finish the meal. Repeat 5-minute breaks every 60 minutes.

## Treatment Fading
- As client successfully eats target foods, the size of bites will gradually be increased to age appropriate size, based on visual inspection of data
- Over repeated successful meals, the reinforcement scheduled will be thinned
- After substantial progress has been made, parents will be directly trained to implement the intervention
  - The BCBA will be present for initial parent training and parent implementation and will fade out until the parents are successfully implementing meals at home, without professional assistance.
- Intervention to be generalized across foods, people, and settings.


## Data
- **Acceptance**
  - **5 seconds:** Record a plus if the client accepts the bite within 5 seconds from presentation
  **OR**
  - **>5 seconds:** Record a plus if the client accepts the bite more than 5 seconds from presentation
- **Result**
  - **Mouth clean:** Record a plus if the client swallows entire bite within 30 seconds from acceptance
  - **Pack:** Record a plus if the client holds food in mouth after 30 seconds from acceptance
- **Feeding behaviors:** Record a plus if the client engages in expel, gag, or vomit behaviors
- **Problem behaviors:** Record each instance of head turns and bats. Take descriptive notes about any other challenging behaviors that occur.

# REFERENCES

American Psychiatric Association (2013). *Diagnostic and statistical manual of mental disorders: DSM-5.* Washington, DC: American Psychiatric Association.

Babbitt, R. L., Hoch, T. A., Coe, D. A., Cataldo, M. F., Kelly, K. J., & Perman, J. A. (1994). Behavioral assessment and treatment of pediatric feeding disorders. *Journal of Developmental & Behavioral Pediatrics, 15*(4), 278–291.

Behavior Analyst Certification Board. (2014). Applied behavior analysis treatment of autism spectrum disorder: Practice guidelines for healthcare funders and managers. Retrieved from: https://bacb.com/wp-content/uploads/2016/08/ABA_Guidelines_for_ASD.pdf.

Behavior Analyst Certification Board. (2016). *Professional and ethical compliance code for behavior analysts.* Retrieved from: https://bacb.com/wp-content/uploads/2016/03/160321-compliance-code-english.pdf.

Clawson, B., Selden, M., Lacks, M., Deaton, A. V., Hall, B., & Bach, R. (2008). Complex pediatric feeding disorders: Using teleconferencing technology to improve access to a treatment program. *Pediatric Nursing, 34*(3), 213.

Cooper, J. O., Heron, T. E., & Heward, W. L. (2007). *Applied behavior analysis.* New York: Prentice Hall.

DeLeon, I. G., & Iwata, B. A. (1996). Evaluation of a multiple-stimulus presentation format for assessing reinforcer preferences. *Journal of Applied Behavior Analysis, 29*(4), 519–533.

Field, D., Garland, M., & Williams, K. (2003). Correlates of specific childhood feeding problems. *Journal of Paediatrics and Child Health, 39*(4), 299–304.

Freeman, K. A., & Piazza, C. C. (1998). Combining stimulus fading, reinforcement, and extinction to treat food refusal. *Journal of Applied Behavior Analysis, 31*(4), 691–694.

Gulotta, C. S., Piazza, C. C., Patel, M. R., & Layer, S. A. (2005). Using food redistribution to reduce packing in children with severe food refusal. *Journal of Applied Behavior Analysis, 38*(1), 39–50.

Hanley, G. P., Iwata, B. A., & McCord, B. E. (2003). Functional analysis of problem behavior: A review. *Journal of Applied Behavior Analysis, 36*(2), 147–185.

Kahng, S., Tarbox, J., & Wilke, A. E. (2001). Use of a multicomponent treatment for food refusal. *Journal of Applied Behavior Analysis, 34*(1), 93–96.

Kanner, L. (1943). Autistic disturbances of affective contact. *Nervous Child, 2,* 217–250.

Kazdin, A. E. (2011). *Single-case research designs: Methods for clinical and applied settings.* New York: Oxford University Press.

Ledford, J. R., & Gast, D. L. (2006). Feeding problems in children with autism spectrum disorders: A review. *Focus on Autism and Other Developmental Disabilities, 21*(3), 153–166.

Luoma, J. B., Hayes, S. C., & Walser, R. D. (2007). *Learning ACT: An acceptance & commitment therapy skills-training manual for therapists.* Oakland, CA: New Harbinger Publications.

Mueller, M. M., Piazza, C. C., Patel, M. R., Kelley, M. E., & Pruett, A. (2004). Increasing variety of foods consumed by blending nonpreferred foods into preferred foods. *Journal of Applied Behavior Analysis, 37*(2), 159–170.

Najdowski, A. C., Tarbox, J., & Wilke, A. E. (2012). Utilizing antecedent manipulations and reinforcement in the treatment of food selectivity by texture. *Education and Treatment of Children*, *35*(1), 101–110.

Najdowski, A. C., Wallace, M. D., Doney, J. K., & Ghezzi, P. M. (2003). Parental assessment and treatment of food selectivity in natural settings. *Journal of Applied Behavior Analysis*, *36*(3), 383–386.

Najdowski, A. C., Wallace, M. D., Penrod, B., Tarbox, J., Reagon, K., & Higbee, T. S. (2008). Caregiver-conducted experimental functional analyses of inappropriate mealtime behavior. *Journal of Applied Behavior Analysis*, *41*(3), 459–465.

National Center for Chronic Disease Prevention and Health Promotion: Division of Population Health. (2014). *Health and academic achievement*. Retrieved from: https://www.cdc.gov/healthyyouth/health_and_academics/pdf/health-academic-achievement.pdf.

Nevin, J. A., & Shahan, T. A. (2011). Behavioral momentum theory: Equations and applications. *Journal of Applied Behavior Analysis*, *44*(4), 877–895.

Penrod, B., Gardella, L., & Fernand, J. (2012). An evaluation of progressive high-probability instructional sequence combined with low-probability demand fading in the treatment of food selectivity. *Journal of Applied Behavior Analysis*, *45*(3), 527–537.

Piazza, C. C., Anderson, C., & Fisher, W. (1993). Teaching self-feeding skills to patients with Rett syndrome. *Developmental Medicine & Child Neurology*, *35*(11), 991–996.

Piazza, C. C., Fisher, W. W., Brown, K. A., Shore, B. A., Patel, M. R., & Blakely-Smith, A. (2003). Functional analysis of inappropriate mealtime behaviors. *Journal of Applied Behavior Analysis*, *36*(2), 187–204.

Piazza, C. C., Patel, M. R., Gulotta, C. S., Sevin, B. M., & Layer, S. A. (2003). On the relative contributions of positive reinforcement and escape extinction in the treatment of food refusal. *Journal of Applied Behavior Analysis*, *36*(3), 309–324.

Reed, G. K., Piazza, C. C., Patel, M. R., Layer, S. A., Bachmeyer, M. H., & Gutshall, K. A. (2004). On the relative contributions of noncontingent reinforcement and escape extinction in the treatment of food refusal. *Journal of Applied Behavior Analysis*, *37*(1), 27–42.

Schreck, K. A., Williams, K., & Smith, A. F. (2004). A comparison of eating behaviors between children with and without autism. *Journal of Autism and Developmental Disorders*, *34*(4), 433–438.

Sharp, W. G. (2016). Assessment of feeding disorders in ASD: A multidisciplinary approach. In J. L. Matson (Ed.), *Handbook of assessment and diagnosis of autism spectrum disorder* (pp. 315–335). Switzerland: Springer International Publishing.

Sharp, W. G., Berry, R. C., McCracken, C., Nuhu, N. N., Marvel, E., & Jaquess, D. L. (2013). Feeding problems and nutrient intake in children with autism spectrum disorders: A meta-analysis and comprehensive review of the literature. *Journal of Autism and Developmental Disorders*, *43*(9), 2159–2173.

Shore, B. A., LeBlanc, D., & Simmons, J. (1999). Reduction of unsafe eating in a patient with esophageal stricture. *Journal of Applied Behavior Analysis*, *32*(2), 225–228.

Stokes, T. F., & Baer, D. M. (1977). An implicit technology of generalization. *Journal of Applied Behavior Analysis*, *10*(2), 349–367.

Tarbox, J., Schiff, A., & Najdowski, A. C. (2010). Parent-implemented procedural modification of escape extinction in the treatment of food selectivity in a young child with autism. *Education and Treatment of Children*, *33*(2), 223–234.

U.S. Department of Health and Human Services and U.S. Department of Agriculture (2015). *2015–2020 Dietary guidelines for Americans*. 8th edition. Retrieved from: http://health.gov/dietaryguidelines/2015/guidelines/.

Wacker, D. P., Lee, J. F., Dalmau, Y. C. P., Kopelman, T. G., Lindgren, S. D., & Waldron, D. B. (2013). Conducting functional communication training via telehealth to reduce the problem behavior of young children with autism. *Journal of Developmental and Physical Disabilities, 25*(1), 35–48.

Williams, K. E., & Foxx, R. M. (2007). *Treating eating problems of children with autism spectrum disorders and developmental disabilities.* Austin, TX: Pro-Ed.

# INDEX

*Note*: Page numbers followed "*f*" refer to figures.